KETOGENIC SLOW
By Jennifer Wittman

Get Back Your Dream Body In Two Weeks! Simple, Quick & Easy,

Copyright 2017 by Jennifer Wittman All rights reserved.

In no way is it legal to reproduce, duplicate, or transmit any part of this document in either electronic means or in printed format. Recording of this publication is strictly prohibited and any storage of this document is not allowed unless with written permission from the publisher. All rights reserved.

The information provided herein is stated to be truthful and consistent, in that any liability, in terms of inattention or otherwise, by any usage or abuse of any policies, processes, or directions contained within is the solitary and utter responsibility of the recipient reader. Under no circumstances will any legal responsibility or blame be held against the publisher for any reparation, damages, or monetary loss due to the information herein, either directly or indirectly.

Respective authors own all copyrights not held by the publisher.

The information herein is offered for informational purposes solely, and is universal as so. The presentation of the information is without contract or any type of guarantee assurance.

The trademarks that are used are without any consent, and the publication of the trademark is without permission or backing by the trademark owner. All trademarks and brands within this book are for clarifying purposes only and are the owned by the owners themselves, not affiliated with this document.

Table of Contents

KETOGENIC SLOW COOKING 1

Introduction 11

SLOW COOKER BENEFITS 13

CHAPTER 1 SLOW COOKING BREAKFAST 15

    Bacon Mushroom Breakfast 15

    Cinnamon Zucchini & Nut Bread 16

    Bacon Cheese & Cauliflower Bake 17

    Spinach Ham Frittata 18

    Delicious Eggplant & Sausage Bake 19

    Garlic Artichoke Hearts Bake 20

    Coconut Spinach Breakfast Casserole 21

    Mapple Ham Breakfast 22

    Sausage Breakfast Casserole 23

    Egg Avocado Breakfast 24

    Ham Cheese Broccoli Brunch Bowl 25

    Spicy Sausage Breakfast Salsa 26

    Mustard Bacon Bell Pepper Casserole 27

    Spinach Tomato Cheesy Frittata 28

    Bacon Garlic Zucchini & Spinach 29

    Maple Pumpkin Nutmeg Bread 30

    Delight Cheddar Hash Brown 31

    Onion Pepperoni Pizza with Meat Crust 32

    Yummy Crock Pot Quiche 33

    Spinach & Sausage Pizza 34

    Garlic Broccoli Cheddar Casserole 35

    Bacon Mushroom Scramble Eggs 36

Cheesy Spanish Omelet 37

Cream Cheese Brussels Sprouts & Italian Sausage Casseroles 38

The Best Meaty Crust Pepperoni Pizza 39

Peppers Onion Sausage Mix Omelet 40

CHAPTER 3: PORK & CHICKEN RECIPES 42

Sour Creamy Chicken 42

Zucchini Lasagne with Minced Pork 43

Garlic Thyme Lemon Chicken 44

BBQ Ribs 45

Oregano Balsamic Chicken 46

Bay Leaf Shoulder Pork Roast 47

Artichoke Chicken Breast Stuffing 48

Butter Lime Pork Chops Salsa 49

Yummy Buffalo Chicken 50

Ginger Turmeric Coconut Pork Curry 51

Butter Cumin Garlic Pork Chops 52

Delicious Spicy Pulled Chicken Breast 53

Chili Pork Leg Roast 54

Tomato Sauce Chili Pulled Pork 55

Onion Pumpkin Curry Chicken 55

Apple Gravy Pork Chops 56

Coconut Sesame Ginger Chicken 57

Chilies Apple Cider Vinegar Chipotle Chicken 58

Cream Cheese Tomato Chicken 60

Garlic Chicken Egg Dish 61

Tasty BabyBack Ribs 62

Bacon-Brussels Sprout Dip 63

Garlic Lemon Cumin Ribs 64

Butter Jalapeno Chicken 65

Thyme Spicy Drumsticks 66

Sweet & Sour Pork Ribs 66

Red Chilies Ginger Mandarin Chicken 68

Yummy Garlic Cauliflower Pork 69

Oregano Paprika Pork Tenderloin 70

Cinnamon Bacon Pork Loin 71

Peanut Spicy Pork Sirloin 72

Ginger Chili Chicken 73

Basil Turkey Meatballs 74

Weekend Beer Chicken 74

Turmeric Coconut Pork Curry 76

Black Olive Italian Chicken 76

CHAPTER 4 : SOUP & STEW RECIPES 78

Veggie Chicken Soup 78

Special One-Pot Meal 79

Ginger Pumpkin Soup 80

Cordon Bleu Chicken Soup 81

Minty-Ball Veggie Soup 83

Sour Cream Beef Meatball Soup 85

Heavy Cream Corned Beef Soup 87

Sausage Lentil Soup 89

Spearmint Lamb Heart and Liver Soup 91

Coriander Cinnamon Broccolic Oxtail Pot 93

Spicy Chorizo Chicken Soup 95

Thyme Garlic Bacon Chicken Chili Soup 96

- Cauliflower Ham Stew 98
- Spicy Onion Turkey 99
- Chilli Turkey Soup 100
- Spicy Rabbit Stew 102
- Delicious Chili Pork Stew 103
- Thyme Celery Bacon Chowder 105
- Almond Curried Chicken Stew 106
- Cumin Chili Beef Tomato Bacon 107
- Simple Seafood Stew 109
- Mustard Sausage Lentil Soup 111
- Delicious Mushroom Chicken Soup 113
- Yello Onion Creamy Chicken Soup 115
- Shallot Mushroom Chowder 116
- Creamy Thyme Chicken Stew 118
- Chili Bell Pepper Sausage Beef 120
- Nutritious Buffalo Chicken Soup 121
- Sweet Potato Sausage Soup 122
- Buttery Red Pepper Soup 123

CHAPTER 5: LAMB & BEEF RECIPES 126
- Shoulder Beef in BBQ Sauce 126
- Malaysian Beef Curry 127
- Rosemary Beef Brisket 128
- Onion Cumin Beef And Cabbage Roast 128
- Garlic Juicy Beef Pot Roast 130
- Broccoli Sesame Coconut Beef 131
- Slow Cooking Balsamic Roast Beef 132
- Coconut Burgundy Beef 133

Green Beans Garlic Minty Lamb 135

Mushroom Beef Stroganoff 136

Mouth-watering Spicy Shredded Beef 137

Chili Spiced Beef Eye Roast 138

Crush Tomatoes Meaty Bolognese 139

Favorite Garlic Bacon & Beef Meatballs 141

Yummy Corned Beef Cabbage Rolls 142

The One-pot Oriental Lamb 144

Thyme Beef Pot Roast 146

CHAPTER 6 DESSERT RECIPES 148

Cranberry-Apple Dessert 148

Pecan Caramel Pudding 149

Chocolate Cake 150

Vanilla Peanut Butter Chocolate Cake 151

Butter Poppy Seed Cake 153

Almond Raspberry Cake 154

Cocoa Chocolate Cake 156

Best Lemon Cake 158

Cream Cheese Pumpkin Cake 159

Dark Chocolate Raspberry Cake 160

Cheesy Red Velvet Cake 161

Coconut Carrot Cake 163

Butter Almond Cocoa Cake 165

Coconut Blueberry Crisp 166

Vanilla Chocolate Cheesecake 168

Double Crème Brûlée 169

Nutmeg Coconut-Peach Cobbler 170

Almond Berry & Coconut Cake 172
Whey Vanilla Pudding Cake 173
Conclusion 176

Introduction

I want to thank you and congratulate you for downloading the book, "KETOGENIC SLOW COOKING: Get Back Your Dream Body In Two Weeks! Simple, Quick & Easy!!".

Your body can be converted from a mainly sugar burning entity into a fat burner with the ketogenic diet. The ketogenic diet is also an innovative way to encourage better general health. There have been numerous people who have turned to this revolutionary diet to attain efficient weight loss due to its characteristic success, and as such it has become exceedingly popular.

Using the ketogenic diet, you'll be able to boost your energy levels through the roof, restore your metabolic health and lose weight in the process. Ketogenic diets utilize low-carb, high-fat foods in conjunction with slow cooker methods which allow your body to reach its maximum potential, and attain the highest grade of health to date.

Rejuvenating your body from the inside out is made simple and easy if you follow the ketogenic diet thoroughly. The damage done to your body from extended exposure to excessive carbohydrates and glucose can be undone with enough patience and perseverance. What healthier way could there be than this diet? After all, there's no price too large to pay for a healthier and stronger body!

Delight your taste buds with carefully selected, slow-cooker recipes, while adhering to a ketogenic nutritional profile at the same time. Save a bunch of time through slow cooking! These recipes are fast to prepare and even easier to make, allowing you the freedom of delicious foods that are healthy at the same time!

Watch the weight wash away, and say hello to a brand new, healthier you!

Thanks again for downloading this book, and I hope you enjoy it!

SLOW COOKER BENEFITS

It's easy to fall in love with the slow cooker and the food you can make from it. Using it is a simple matter of setting the ingredients into the pot in the morning and coming back home to a fully cooked, delicious lunch or dinner! Otherwise, how does a ready-made breakfast after a rough night sound to you? Great, right? You can make this happen by setting the slow cooker right before you go to sleep, and wake up to a perfect meal in the morning or afternoon. For more time saving, you can also prep your meals in the evening, and stick them in the fridge, ready for morning use. Here are some other advantages.

Time Efficient – The slow cooker doesn't need to be minded at all throughout the course of cooking. All you need to do is prep the food to begin with and let the cooker do its thing.

Compact – The pots used for slow cooking are small and convenient, excellent for when you need to carry meals to and from a place. Most also have excellent insulation to keep food warm throughout the journey.

Delicious Meals – Slow cookers cook fresh ingredients over an extended period of time, so the nutritional value of such cooked foods are maintained to an excellent degree.

Power Saving – If you're someone who wants to cut back on energy bills, then the slow cooker is your best friend. Much less energy consumptive compared to an oven, and when in use, can use as little electricity as a 100-watt light bulb.

Produces Little Heat – Following on from low energy consumption, the amount of excess heat is low. Especially during sweltering summer months, this quality is highly convenient.

Easy Cooking of Tough Meat Cuts – Slow cookers use contained moisture to help break down tougher parts of the meat as well as retaining the juicy texture you can find in top end restaurants.

Can work Unattended – The cooker uses negligible energy, and thus there's little danger to leaving it on when you go on outings. No supervision required!

Easy Cleaning – There's only one pot to wash after everything is said and done. Add any utensils used in the meal prep to the wash load and you'll have a sparkling kitchen in no time flat!

CHAPTER 1 SLOW COOKING BREAKFAST

Bacon Mushroom Breakfast

Ingredients

2 cups cooked ground sausage
1/2 cup chopped onion
1 Tbs dried parsley
1 tsp garlic powder
1 tsp thyme
6 cooked, drained, crumbled bacon slices

2 cups organic chicken broth

1 cup chopped red bell pepper

1/2 cup Parmesan cheese

1 cups heavy white cream

2 cups sliced, raw mushrooms

salt and pepper to taste

Directions

1. Add all ingredients to a large Slow Cooker.
2. Cook on LOW mode for 4-6 hour. Make sure not to overcook or cook at too high a heat or the cream will separate. Serve hot.

Nutrition Facts :
Carbs: 2,14g , Fat: 15,52g ,Calories: 166; Fiber: 0,31g, Protein: 6,73g

Cinnamon Zucchini & Nut Bread

Ingredients:

2 cups shredded zucchini
½ cup ground walnuts
1 cup ground almonds
1/3 cup coconut flakes
2 teaspoons cinnamon
½ teaspoon baking soda
1 ½ teaspoons baking powder
½ teaspoon salt
3 large eggs
⅓ cup softened coconut oil
1 cup sweetener, Swerve (or suitable substitute)
2 teaspoons vanilla

Directions:

1. Shred the zucchini and ground the walnuts.
2. In a bowl, beat the eggs, oil, sweetener, and vanilla together.
3. Add the dry ingredients to the wet mixture.
4. Fold in the zucchini and walnuts.
5. Pour the batter into a bread pan, which fits inside the crock-pot.
6. Crumble aluminium foil into four balls, place on bottom of the crock-pot and set the pan in the crock-pot with a paper towel on top to absorb the water.
7. Cover, cook on high for 3 hours. Cool, wrap in foil and refrigerate.

Nutritional facts: net Carb 4g; Protein 5g; F at 18g Carlories 210g Serve cold with tea or coffee.

Bacon Cheese & Cauliflower Bake

Ingredients:

1 head cauliflower, cut into florets
½ cup cream cheese
¼ cup whipping cream
2 Tablespoons lard (or butter, if you prefer)
1 Tablespoon lard (or butter, if you prefer) to grease the crock-pot
1 teaspoon salt
½ teaspoon fresh ground black pepper
½ cup yellow cheese, Cheddar, shredded
6 slices of bacon, crisped and crumbled

Directions:

1. Grease the crock-pot.
2. Add all the ingredients, except the cheese and the bacon.
3. Cook on low for 3 hours.
4. Open the lid and add cheese. Re-cover, cook for an additional hour.
5. Top with the bacon and serve.

Nutritional facts: *net Carb 3g; Protein 11g; Fat 20g* , **Calories: 232**
Good for brunch with a couple cherry tomatoes and avocado slices.

Spinach Ham Frittata

Calories: 109
Total Fat: 6.9 g
Total Carbs: 1.8 g
Dietary Fiber: 1 g

Ingredients:
- 10 eggs, large-sized
- 1/2 green bell pepper, diced
- 1 cup ham, diced
- 2 handfuls fresh spinach
- Salt and pepper

Equipment:
- 1 slow cooker liner

Directions:

1. Line a 6-quart, oval-shaped slow cooker with the liner and grease with nonstick cooking spray.
2. Put the ham, spinach, and peppers into the slow cooker.
3. Crack the eggs into a bowl. Add the pepper, salt, and whisk until completely scrambled. Pour the beaten eggs into the slow cooker.
4. Close the lid of the cooker and cook for 1 1/2-2 hours on HIGH or until the center of the frittata no longer jiggles when you shake the slow cooker.
5. Lift out the slow cooker pot and slide out the liner with a spatula. Slice the frittata into squares and serve.

Delicious Eggplant & Sausage Bake

Ingredients:

2 cups eggplant, cubed, salted and drained
1 Tablespoon olive oil
2.2 pounds spicy pork sausage
1 Tablespoon Worcestershire sauce
1 Tablespoon mustard
2 regular cans Italian diced tomatoes
1 jar tomato pasta
2 cups mozzarella cheese, shredded

Directions:

1. Grease the crock pot with olive oil.
2. Mix the sausage, Worcestershire sauce, and mustard. Pour the mixture in the crock-pot.
3. Top the meat mixture with eggplant.
4. Pour the tomatoes over the mixture, sprinkle with grated cheese.
5. Cover, cook on low for 4 hours.

Nutritional values per serving: net Carb 6g; Protein 15g; Calories 210, Fat: 12g
Enjoy for brunch with avocado slices.

Garlic Artichoke Hearts Bake

Ingredients:

1 cup Cheddar cheese, grated
½ cup dry Parmesan cheese
1 cup cream cheese
1 cup spinach, chopped
1 clove of garlic, crushed
1 jar artichoke hearts, chopped
Salt and pepper to taste

Directions:

1. Place all the ingredients in the crock-pot. Mix lightly.
2. Cover, cook on high for 2 hours.

Nutritional values per serving: net Carb 3g; Protein 10g; Calories: 209, Fat 10g
Serve with nut crackers and cherry tomatoes.

Coconut Spinach Breakfast Casserole

Ingredients:

Eggs – 8
Silk almond milk (unsweetened) – ¾ cup
Fresh spinach (chopped) – 5 oz.
Artichoke hearts (chopped) – 6 oz.
Parmesan cheese (grated) – 1 cup
Garlic cloves (minced) – 3 cups
Salt – 1 teaspoon
Pepper – ½ teaspoon
Coconut flour – ¾ cup
Baking powder – 1 tablespoon

Directions:

1. Whisk together all the ingredients in a bowl and pour the mixture into a greased slow cooker.
2. Cook covered for 4-6 hours on low.

Nutrition facts:: 141 Cal, 7.1 g total fat, 3.79 g net carb., 3.97 g fiber, 9.98 g protein.

Mapple Ham Breakfast

Ingredients:

Boneless ham (fully cooked) – 5 lbs.
Maple syrup – ½ cup
Honey Dijon mustard – ½ cup
Packed brown sugar – ½ cup

Directions:

1. Using a knife, make diagonal shaped cross pattern on the ham and place it in a slow cooker.
2. Whisk together the rest of the ingredients and pour it over the ham.
3. Cook covered for 3-4 hours on low.
4. Remove the ham, and cover with a foil for 10 minutes.
5. Slice and serve.

Nutrition facts:: 430 Cal, 24 g fat (8 g sat. fat),   0 g fiber, 32 g protein.

Sausage Breakfast Casserole

Ingredients:

Eggs - 8
Milk (low-fat) – 1 ½ cups
Bulk sausage (cooked, drained) – 1 lb.
Jalapeno (seeded, chopped) – 1
Red bell pepper (chopped) – 1
Green onions (sliced) – ¾ cup
Mexican blend cheese (low-fat) – 2 cups
Corn tortillas – 9
Salsa – ½ cup

Directions:

1. Whisk together the milk, jalapeno and eggs.
2. Mix together the red bell pepper, sausage, green onions and cheese in a bowl.
3. Spread 3 tortillas on the bottom of a greased slow cooker.
4. Spread a layer of the sausage mixture and then cover with another 3 tortillas.
5. Repeat the layering one more time and then finally pour the egg mix over.
6. Cook covered for 4-5 hours on low until the center is set.
7. Serve with the salsa.

Nutrition facts: 386 Cal, 24 g total fat 2.6 g fiber, 24.7 g protein.

Egg Avocado Breakfast

Calories: 268
Total Fat: 2.4 g
Protein: 7.5 g;
Total Carbs: 9 g
Dietary Fiber: 6.7 g

Ingredients:

- 2 eggs
- 1 avocado, large-sized
- Cracked black pepper

Directions:

1. Set the slow cooker to HIGH. Lay a sheet of baking paper in the bottom of the cooker.
2. Cut the avocado into half and remove the seed. With the cut side facing up, put the avocado in the baking paper. Carefully crack 1 egg into the seed-hollowed part of each avocado half. Sprinkle with black pepper to taste.
3. Close the lid of the cooker and cook for 45 minutes on HIGH or until the eggs are cooked to your liking.

Ham Cheese Broccoli Brunch Bowl

Ingredients:

1 medium head of broccoli, chopped small

4 cups vegetable broth

2 Tablespoons olive oil

1 teaspoon mustard seeds, ground

3 garlic cloves, minced

Salt and pepper to taste

2 cups Cheddar cheese, shredded

2 cups ham, cubed

Pinch of paprika

Directions:

1. Add all ingredients to the crock-pot in order of the list.

2. Cover, cook on low for 8 hours.

Nutritional facts: net Carb 8g; Protein 25g; Fat 28g Calories : 290

Serve with tomato slices and black olives.

Spicy Sausage Breakfast Salsa

Ingredients:

Pork sausage roll (cooked, sliced) - 1 (12 oz)

Eggs – 10

Garlic powder – ½ teaspoon

Coriander – ½ teaspoon

Cumin – 1 teaspoon

Chili powder – 1 teaspoon

Salt – ¼ teaspoon

Pepper – ¼ teaspoon

Salsa – 1 cup

Milk (1%) – 1 cup

Pepper Jack cheese – 1 cup

Directions:

1. Cook the pork sausage over medium heat in a skillet until browned then add in salsa and seasonings.

2. Set aside until slightly cooled.

3. Whisk the milk and eggs in a bowl then add in the pork. Add in cheese after and stir until well combined.

4. Grease a slow cooker and add in the mixture, cover and cook on low for five hours or on high for two and a half hours.

5. Garnish as desired and enjoy the meal.

Nutrition facts : 320 Cal, 24.1 g total fat , 5.2 g carb., 0.8 g fiber, 17.9 g protein.

Mustard Bacon Bell Pepper Casserole
Ingredients:

Bulk breakfast sausage – ½ lb.

Bacon (chopped) – 6 oz.

Yellow onion (diced) – ½ cup

White sweet potatoes (peeled, shredded) – 1 lb.

Red bell pepper (seeded, diced) – 1

Orange bell pepper (seeded, diced) - 1

Eggs (beaten) – 16

Almond milk – ½ cup

Sea salt – 1 teaspoon

Coconut milk (full-fat) – ¼ cup

Dry mustard – ¾ teaspoon

Cracked bell pepper – ¼ teaspoon

Ghee – for greasing

Directions:

1. Cook the onion, bacon and sausage in a skillet for 10-12 minutes.

2. Grease a slow cooker with ghee and press the sweet potato onto its base.

3. Spread the onion mix ad bell peppers over.

4. Whisk together the rest of the ingredients and pour it into the slow cooker.

5. Cook for 6-8 hours on low.

Nutrition facts : 375 Cal, 28.4 g total 8.2 g carb., 1.1 g fiber, 21.2 g protein.

Spinach Tomato Cheesy Frittata

Ingredients:

Extra-virgin olive oil – 1 tablespoon

Onion (diced) - ½ cup

Mozzarella cheese (2%, shredded) – 1 cup

Eggs – 3

Egg whites – 3

1% Milk – 2 tablespoons

Black pepper – ¼ teaspoon

White pepper - ¼ teaspoon

Baby spinach (chopped) – 1 cup

Roma tomato (diced) - 1

Salt – to taste

Directions:

1. Sauté the onions in a pan for 5 minutes.

2. Place the onions in a bowl and whisk in the rest of the ingredients except ¼ cup cheese.

3. Transfer the mixture into a greased slow cooker and sprinkle the rest of the cheese on top.

4. Cook for 1 – 1 ½ hours on low until set.

Nutrition Information per serving: 139 Cal, 8 g total fat , 4 g carb., 1 g fiber, 12 g protein.

Bacon Garlic Zucchini & Spinach

Ingredients:

8 slices bacon

1 Tablespoon olive oil

4 medium zucchini, cubed

2 cups baby spinach

1 red onion, diced

6 garlic cloves, sliced thin

1 cup chicken broth

Salt and pepper to taste

Directions:

1. In a pan, heat the olive oil, brown the bacon for 5 minutes. Break it in pieces in the pan.

2. Place remaining ingredients in crock-pot, pour the bacon and fat from pan over the ingredients.

3. Cover, cook on low for 6 hours.

Nutritional values per serving: net Carb 7g; Protein 13g; Fat 12g , Calories : 210

Serve as a side dish to any meat.

Maple Pumpkin Nutmeg Bread

Ingredients:

100% apple juice – ¾ cup

Dried apple juice sweetened cranberries – ½ cup

Coconut flour – 1 ¾ cups

Maple sugar flakes – ½ cup

Baking powder – 2 teaspoons

Nutmeg (ground) – 1 teaspoon

Baking soda – ¼ teaspoon

Ground all spice – ¼ teaspoon

Sea salt - ¼ teaspoon

Pumpkin (cooked, pureed) – 1 cup

Plain Greek yoghurt (non-fat) – ½ cup

Egg whites - 4

Safflower oil – ¼ cup

Vanilla extract – 1 tablespoon

Pecan pieces (unsalted, toasted) – 2 oz.

Directions:-

1. Mix together the cranberries and apple juice in a saucepan and bring to boil. Leave aside for 10 minutes.
2. Mix together all the dry ingredients in a bowl.
3. In another bowl, mix together all the wet ingredients including the cranberry mix.
4. Add the wet ingredients to the dry along with the pecans and mix well.
5. Transfer the mixture into a greased loaf pan.
6. Place in a slow cooker on a rack.
7. Cook for 2 hours 45 minutes on high.

Nutrition facts: 159 Cal, 25 g total fat (1 g sat. fat), 70 mg sodium, 21 g carb., 3 g fiber, 4 g protein.

Delight Cheddar Hash Brown

Ingredients:

Frozen hash browns (shredded) – 20 oz.
Thick cut bacon (cooked, chopped) – 8 slices
Cheddar cheese (shredded) – 8 oz.
Green onions (thinly sliced) – 6
Eggs – 12
Milk – ½ cup
Salt – ½ teaspoon
Pepper – ¼ teaspoon

Directions:

1. Grease a slow cooker with oil and layer hash browns, bacon, cheese and green onions, repeating the layering another time.
2. Whisk together the rest of the ingredients and pour over.
3. Cook for 2 - 3 hours on high.

Nutrition Facts : 342 Cal, 22 g total fat, 14 g carb., 2 g fiber, 21 g protein.

Onion Pepperoni Pizza with Meat Crust

List of Ingredients:

2.2. pounds lean ground beef

2 garlic cloves, minced

1 Tablespoon dry, fried onions

Salt and pepper to taste

2 cups shredded mozzarella

1 ¾ cup sugarless ready-made pizza sauce

2 cups shredded yellow cheese, Cheddar

½ cup sliced pepperoni

Directions:

1. In a pan, brown the beef with the seasoning together.
2. Mix the beef with the cheese.
3. Butter the crock-pot and spread the crust out evenly over the bottom.
4. Pour the pizza sauce over the crust and spread evenly.
5. Top with the cheese and arrange the pepperoni slices.
6. Cover, cook on low for 4 hours.

Nutritional values per serving: net Carb 5g; Protein 46g; Fat 22g , Calories: 310

Serve with cucumber slices sprinkled with fresh chopped dill, Himalayan salt and olive oil.

Yummy Crock Pot Quiche

Ingredients:

1 Tablespoon butter
10 eggs, beaten
1 cup heavy cream
1 cup Cheddar cheese, shredded
Pinch fresh ground black pepper
10 strips of bacon, crisped and crumbled
½ cup fresh spinach, chopped

Directions:

1. Butter the crock-pot.
2. In a large bowl, mix all the ingredients, except bacon crumbles.
3. Transfer mixture to the crock-pot, sprinkle bacon on top.
4. Cover, cook on low for 4 hours. (In the last 15 minutes watch carefully, not to overcook it.)

Nutritional values per serving: net Carb 2g; Proein 15g; Fat 28g, Calories: 310

Serve with tomato slices sprinkled with fresh chopped parsley, Himalayan salt and olive oil.

Spinach & Sausage Pizza

Ingredients:
1 Tablespoon olive oil
1 cup lean ground beef
2 cups spicy pork sausage
2 garlic cloves, minced
1 Tablespoon dry, fried onions
Salt and pepper to taste
1 ¾ cups sugarless ready-made pizza sauce
3 cups fresh spinach
½ cup sliced pepperoni
¼ cup pitted black olives, sliced
¼ cup sun-dried tomatoes, chopped
½ cup spring onions, chopped
3 cups shredded mozzarella

Directions:
1. In a pan, heat the olive oil. Brown the beef, then the pork. Drain the oil off both meats, mix together.
2. Pour the meat in the crock-pot. Spread evenly and press down.
3. Alternate in layers: pizza sauce, toppings, and cheese.
4. Cover and cook on low for 4-6 hours.

Nutritional values per serving: net Cabr 5g; P rotein 30g; Fat 25g, Calories : 350

Serve with pickles.

Garlic Broccoli Cheddar Casserole

Ingredients:

Broccoli head (chopped) – 1
Jones Dairy Farm Little Links (cooked, sliced) – 1 (12 oz) package
Cheddar (shredded) – 1 cup
Eggs – 10
Whipping cream – ¾ cup
Garlic cloves (minced) – 2
Salt – ½ teaspoon
Pepper – ¼ teaspoon

Directions:

1. Grease a slow cooker and layer half the broccoli, sausage and cheese.
2. Repeat the layering with the remaining broccoli, sausage and cheese.
3. Whisk together the rest of the ingredients and pour over the layerings.
4. Cook for 4-5 hours on low.

Nutrition Information per serving: 384 Cal, 28 g total fat, , 1.18 g fiber, 26.13 g protein.

Bacon Mushroom Scramble Eggs

Ingredients:

Bacon slices - 8
Fresh mushrooms (sliced) – 8 oz.
Butter – 3 tablespoons
Eggs – 16
Milk – 1 cup
Salt – ½ teaspoon
Pepper – ¼ teaspoon
Condensed cream of mushroom soup – 10 ¾ oz
Fresh chives (chopped) – 2 tablespoons
Italian plum tomatoes (sliced) - 4
Cheddar cheese (shredded) – 2 cups

Directions:

1. Cook the bacon in a skillet and then crumble it. Place aside.
2. Cook the mushrooms in the bacon drippings for 5 minutes. Place aside.
3. Melt the butter in the skillet.
4. Whisk together the milk, eggs, salt and pepper and add cook it in the skillet, stirring occasionally until firm, but yet moist. Mix in the chives and soup.
5. Place a layer of the egg mix in a slow cooker, followed by a layer mushrooms, tomatoes, Cheddar cheese and bacon.
6. Repeat the layering once more.
7. Cook covered for 30 minutes on low.

Nutrition facts : 390 Cal, 22 g total fat , 0 g fiber, 17 g protein.

Cheesy Spanish Omelet

Ingredients:

Eggs (lightly beaten) – 12
Russet potatoes (peeled, chopped) – 1 lb
Onion (chopped) – ½ cup
Olive oil – 2 tablespoon
Salt – ¾ teaspoon
Black pepper – ¼ teaspoon
Cheddar cheese (reduced-fat, shredded) – ½ cup
Tomato (chopped) – ½ cup

Directions:

1. Grease a slow cooker lined with a disposable liner.
2. Lightly brown the potatoes in a skillet for 5 minutes.
3. Mix in the onions and cook for another 2-3 minutes.
4. Transfer the onion-potato mix to the slow cooker, spreading it evenly and season with salt and pepper.
5. Whisk the eggs and pour it over the onion-potato mix, stirring gently to spread.
6. Cook covered for 2 ½ hours on low.
7. Transfer the omelet onto a platter and sprinkle the cheese on top.
8. Keep covered for 5 minutes until the cheese melts.
9. Serve topped with the tomato.

Nutrition Information per serving: 202 Cal, 12 g total fat , 11 g carb., 1 g fiber, 12 g protein.

Cream Cheese Brussels Sprouts & Italian Sausage Casseroles

Ingredients :

8 eggs

2 cups Brussels sprouts

2 links Italian sausages, sliced

1/2 cup shredded Cheddar, divide

2 cloves garlic, minced

3/4 cup cream cheese

salt and fresh ground pepper to taste

ghee or lard

Directions :

1. Grease your Slow cooker with ghee or lard.

2. In a bowl, whisk eggs, cream cheese, garlic, salt and pepper to taste. Combine all well. Pour over layered ingredients.

3. Layer one half of the Brussels sprouts, half of the sausage and half of the cheese into the slow cooker. Repeat with remaining Brussels sprouts, sausage and cheese.

4. Cook on LOW for 4 to 5 hours or HIGH for 2 to 3 hours. Serve hot.

Nutrition Facts: Calories 270, Fat 18g   Carbs: 6.72g ,Fiber: 1.15g ,Protein: 18g

The Best Meaty Crust Pepperoni Pizza

Ingredients:

2.2. pounds lean ground beef

2 garlic cloves, minced

1 Tablespoon dry, fried onions

Salt and pepper to taste

2 cups shredded mozzarella

1 ¾ cup sugarless ready-made pizza sauce

2 cups shredded yellow cheese, Cheddar

½ cup sliced pepperoni

Directions:

1. In a pan, brown the beef with the seasoning together.

2. Mix the beef with the cheese.

3. Butter the crock-pot and spread the crust out evenly over the bottom.

4. Pour the pizza sauce over the crust and spread evenly.

5. Top with the cheese and arrange the pepperoni slices.

6. Cover, cook on low for 4 hours.

Nutritional values per serving: net Carb 5g; Protein 46g; Fat 25g , Calories: 320

Serve with cucumber slices sprinkled with fresh chopped dill, Himalayan salt and olive oil.

Peppers Onion Sausage Mix Omelet

Ingredients :

8 eggs

1/2 lb pork sausage, cooked

1 cup red peppers, diced

green peppers, diced

1 cup yellow peppers, diced

1 cup shredded Cheddar cheese (optional)

1/2 cup chopped green onions

1/4 cup heavy cream

1/2 tsp crushed red pepper flakes

salt and freshly ground black pepper to taste

ghee butter coconut oil (optional)

Directions :

1. Grease and line sides of Slow Cooker with foil.

2. In a bowl, whisk beat eggs, milk cream, pepper flakes, salt and pepper to taste.

3. Layer in a bottom sausages and diced peppers mix.

4. Pour the egg mixture over the the sausages and peppers.

5. Cover and cook on LOW setting 4 to 5 hours, or on HIGH heat for 2 1/2 to 3 hours.

6. When ready, sprinkle with shredded cheese (optional) and green onions over top of casserole.

7. Cover and cook 10 minutes more.

8. Serve hot.

Nutrition Facts :Calories: 245, Fat: 19g, Carbs: 3g Fiber: 0,5g Protein: 14,36g

CHAPTER 3: PORK & CHICKEN RECIPES

Sour Creamy Chicken

Ingredients:

Sour cream – 1 cup

Chicken stock – ½ cup

Diced tomatoes and green chilies – 1 (14 oz.) can

Homemade taco seasoning – 1 batch

Chicken breast – 2 lbs.

Directions:-
1. Combine all the ingredients in the slow cooker.
2. Cook for 6 hours on low.

Nutrition Information per serving: 262 Cal, 13 g total fat, 2.5 g fiber, 32 g protein.

Zucchini Lasagne with Minced Pork

Ingredients:
4 medium-sized zucchini
1 small onion, diced
1 garlic clove, minced
2 cups lean ground pork, minced
2 regular cans diced Italian tomatoes
2 Tablespoons olive oil
2 cups grated Mozzarella cheese
1 egg
Small bunch of fresh basil or 1 Tablespoon dry basil
Salt and pepper to taste
2 Tablespoons butter to grease crock-pot

Directions:
1. Cut the zucchini lengthwise making 6 slices from each vegetable. Salt and let drain. Discard the liquid.
2. In a pan, heat the olive oil. Sauté the onion and garlic for 5 minutes.
3. Add minced meat and cook for another 5 minutes. Add tomatoes and simmer for another 5 minutes.
4. Add seasoning and mix well. Add basil leaves. Cool slightly.
5. Beat the egg, mix in 1 cup of cheese.
6. Grease the crock-pot with butter and start layering the lasagne. First, the zucchini slices, then a layer of meat mixture, top it with cheese, and repeat. Finish with zucchini and the second cup of cheese.
7. Cover, cook on low for 8 hours.

Nutritional values per serving: net Carb 10g; Protein 23g; Fat 30g, Calories: 398

Serve with green salad and vinaigrette dressing – pink Himalayan salt, olive oil and vinegar.

Garlic Thyme Lemon Chicken

Ingredients:

Garlic cloves – 10-15
Sliced lemons – 2
Ground black pepper – ½ teaspoon
Thyme – 1 teaspoon
Whole chicken (inside cleaned) – 3 ½ pounds

Directions:

1. Place the garlic and the lemon at the base of a slow cooker.
2. Combine all the spices and season the chicken with it inside out.
3. Place the chicken in the slow cooker.
4. Cook covered for 4 hours on low.
5. Leave to stand for 15 minutes and then carve.

Nutrition facts: 120 Cal, 8 g total fat , 1 g carb., 0g fiber, 12 g protein.

BBQ Ribs

Ingredients:

3 pounds pork ribs
1 Tablespoon of olive oil
1 small can ounces tomato paste – 28 fl ounces
½ cup hot water
½ cup vinegar
6 Tablespoons Worcestershire sauce
4 Tablespoons dry mustard
1 Tablespoon chilli powder
1 heaping teaspoon ground cumin
1 teaspoon powdered Swerve (or suitable substitute)
Salt and pepper to taste

Directions:

1. In a frying pan, heat the olive oil. Brown the ribs on both sides.
2. Add them to the crock-pot.
3. Combine remaining ingredients in a bowl, blend well. Pour over the ribs - coat all sides.
4. Cover, cook on low for 8 hours.

Nutritional values per serving: net Carb 14g; Protein38; Fat 28g, Calories: 410

Serve with avocado cubes marinated in olive oil, salt and fresh chopped dill.

Oregano Balsamic Chicken

Ingredients:

Skinless, boneless chicken breasts – 6
Diced tomatoes – 2 (14.5 oz.) can
Thinly sliced onion – 1
Garlic cloves – 4
Balsamic vinegar – ½ cup
Olive oil – 1 tablespoon
Dried oregano – 1 teaspoon
Dried rosemary - 1 teaspoon
Dried basil – 1 teaspoon
Thyme – ½ teaspoon
Ground black pepper – To taste
Salt – To taste

Directions:

1. Combine all the ingredients in a slow cooker.
2. Cook covered for 4 hours on high.

Nutrition Information per serving: 190 Cal, 6 g total fat, 5 g carb., 1 g fiber, 26 g protein.

Bay Leaf Shoulder Pork Roast

Ingredients:

3 pounds pork shoulder, whole
1 can Italian diced tomatoes
1 sweet onion, diced
3 garlic cloves, diced
4 Tablespoons lard
1 cup water
1 bay leaf
¼ teaspoon ground cloves
Salt and pepper to taste

Directions:

1. Place meat in crock-pot, pour water and tomatoes over it, so the liquid covers 1/3 of the meat.
2. Add remaining ingredients.
3. Cover, cook on low for 8 hours.

Nutritional values per serving: net Carb 10g; Protein 33g; Fat 30g, Calories: 421
Serve with avocado slices and grated Parmesan.

Artichoke Chicken Breast Stuffing

Ingredients:

Spinach (chopped finely) – 3 cups
Roasted red peppers (chopped) – ½ cup
Black olives (sliced) - - ¼ cup
Canned artichoke hearts (chopped) – 1 cup
Reduced-fat feta cheese – 4 oz.
Dried oregano -1 teaspoon
Garlic powder – 1 teaspoon
Chicken broth (low-sodium) – 1 ½ cups
Salt and pepper – to taste

Directions:

1. Season the chicken with salt and pepper and make a deep cut at the center.
2. Mix together the artichoke hearts, spinach, peppers, oregano, feta and garlic.
3. Stuff the mixture into the chicken pockets and place in the slow cooker.
4. Cook for 4 hours on low.

Nutrition Information per serving: 222 Cal, 7 g total fat, 4 g net carb., 4 g fiber, 36 g protein.

Butter Lime Pork Chops Salsa

Ingredients:

Pork sirloin chops (bone-in) – 3.32 lbs.
Butter – 3 tablespoons
Salsa – ½ cup
Lime juice – 5 tablespoons
Ground cumin – ½ teaspoon
Garlic powder – ¾ teaspoon
Salt – ¾ teaspoon
Black pepper – ¾ teaspoon

Directions:
1. Combine all the spices and mix well.
2. Season the pork with the spice mixture.
3. Melt the butter in a pan and lightly brown the pork chops in it on both sides.
4. Place the pork in a slow cooker.
5. Mix together the lime juice and salsa and add it over the pork.
6. Cook covered for 3-4 hours on high.

Nutrition Information per serving: 364 Cal, 17 g total fat, , 3 g carb., 0 g fiber, 51 g protein.

Yummy Buffalo Chicken

Ingredients:

Chicken breasts (frozen) - 6
Franks Red hot – 1 bottle
Hidden valley ranch – ½ packet
Butter – 3 tablespoon

Directions:

1. Combine all the ingredients except the butter in a slow
2. Cook covered for 6 hours on low.
3. Shred the chicken and mix in the butter.
4. Cook uncovered for another hour on low.

Nutrition Information per serving: 297 Cal, 8 g total fat, 1 g carb., 0 g fiber, 52 g protein.

Ginger Turmeric Coconut Pork Curry

Ingredients:

2.2 pounds pork shoulder, cubed
1 Tablespoon coconut oil
1 yellow onion, diced
2 garlic cloves, minced
2 Tablespoons tomato paste
1 small can coconut milk – 12 fl ounces
1 cup water
½ cup white wine
1 teaspoon turmeric
1 teaspoon ginger powder
1 teaspoon curry powder
½ teaspoon paprika
Salt and pepper to taste

Directions:

1. In a pan, heat 1 tablespoon olive oil. Sauté the onion and garlic for 2-3 minutes.
2. Add the pork and brown it. Finish with tomato paste.
3. In the crock-pot, mix all remaining ingredients, submerge the meat in the liquid.
4. Cover, cook on low for 8 hours.

Nutritional values per serving: net Carb 7g; Protein 30g; F 31g , Calories: 425

Serve with sour cream and cucumber cubes sprinkled with fresh chopped dill.

Butter Cumin Garlic Pork Chops

Ingredients:

Pork Sirloin Chops (bone-in) – 3.32 lbs.
Salsa – ½ cup
Butter – 3 tablespoon
Lime juice – 5 tablespoon
Ground cumin – ½ teaspoon
Garlic powder – ¾ teaspoon
Salt – ¾ teaspoon
Black pepper - ¾ teaspoon

Directions:

1. Mix together all the spices and rub it on the chops.
2. Melt the butter in a pan and brown the chops in it for 2 ½ minutes per side.
3. Transfer the chops into the slow cooker and pour the salsa over.
4. Cook for 3-4 hours on high.

Nutrition Information per serving: 364 Cal, 17 g total fat, 3 g carb., 0 g fiber, 51 g protein.

Delicious Spicy Pulled Chicken Breast

Ingredients:

1 teaspoon dry oregano
1 teaspoon dry thyme
1 teaspoon dried rosemary
1 teaspoon garlic powder
1 teaspoon sweet paprika
½ teaspoon chilli powder
Salt and pepper to taste
4 tablespoons butter
5.5 pounds chicken breasts
1 ½ cups ready-made tomato salsa
2 Tablespoons of olive oil

Directions:

1. Mix dry seasoning, sprinkle half on the bottom of crock-pot.
2. Place the chicken breasts over it, sprinkle rest of spices.
3. Pour the salsa over the chicken.
4. Cover, cook on low for 6 hours.

Nutritional facts : net Carb 3g; Protein 57g; Fat: 22g, Calories :359

Serve over steamed and buttered broccoli florets.

Chili Pork Leg Roast

Ingredients:

8 pounds pork leg
1 Tablespoon butter
1 yellow onion, sliced
6 garlic cloves, peeled and minced
2 Tablespoons ground cumin
2 Tablespoons ground thyme
2 Tablespoons ground chilli
1 teaspoon salt
1 teaspoon fresh ground black pepper
1 cup hot water

Directions:

1. Butter the crock-pot. Slice criss-crosses along top of pork leg.
2. Arrange onion slices and minced garlic along the bottom of the crock-pot.
3. Place meat on top of vegetables.
4. In a small bowl, mix the herbs. Rub it all over the pork leg.
5. Add the water. Cover, cook on high for 8 hours.
6. Remove from crock pot, place on a platter, cover with foil. Let it rest for 1 hour.
7. Shred the meat and serve.

Nutritional values per serving: net Carb 0g; Protein 8g; Fat 11g , Calories: 260

Serve with creamed green beans, sprinkled with fresh Parmesan cheese.

Tomato Sauce Chili Pulled Pork

Ingredients:

4 lb. pork shoulder, fat trimmed
28 oz. tomato sauce
3 Tbsp. onion powder
1 Tbsp. cumin
2 tsp. cinnamon
2 tsp. chili powder
½ tsp. cayenne pepper
½ tsp. salt

Directions:

1. Combine tomato sauce and spices in a bowl.
2. Arrange pork in slow cooker, and pour sauce on top.
3. Cover and cook on low for 5-7 hours. Pork is done when it shreds easily with a fork.

Nutritional Info Per Serving:
Calories 441, Carbs 4 g, Fat 26 g, Protein 45 g

Onion Pumpkin Curry Chicken

Ingredients:

Chicken (cubed) – 1 lb.
Curry paste – 2 tablespoon
Onion (sliced finely) – 1
Pumpkin (cubed) – 14 oz.
Coconut cream – 1 1/3 cups
Fresh spinach (chopped) – 14 oz.
Cashews - for garnish

Directions:

1. Combine all the ingredients in a slow cooker except the spinach and cashews.
2. Cook for 4-6 hours on high.
3. Add the spinach 10 minutes prior serving and stir well.
4. Serve the curry garnished with cashews.

Nutrition Information per serving : 347 Cal, 21.9 g total fat, 9.5 g carb., 3.5g fiber, 29.2 g protein.

Apple Gravy Pork Chops

Ingredients:

24 oz. boneless pork chops

1 tsp. salt

1 tsp. pepper

1 tsp. garlic powder

1 tsp. onion powder

1 tsp. dried oregano

3 Tbsp. almond flour, plus 2 tsp.

2 Tbsp. coconut oil

1 c. chicken broth

½ c. onion, chopped

½ Granny Smith apple, chopped

½ c. water

Directions:

1. In a small bowl, combine salt, pepper, garlic powder, onion powder and dried oregano. Rub spice mix onto each pork chop, seasoning liberally. If necessary, add more spices to coat thoroughly.

2. Dust pork chops (both sides) with 2 teaspoons almond flour.

3. In a large skillet, heat oil over medium-high heat. Sear pork chops for about 4-5 minutes on each side.

4. While pork chops are searing, whisk together chicken broth and remaining almond flour.

5. Remove pork chops to slow cooker. In the same skillet, sauté chopped onion and apple.

6. After about 5 minutes, add chicken broth mixture to pan. Allow to thicken for 2-3 minutes, then remove from heat.

7. Pour gravy and ½ cup of water over pork chops. Cover and cook on high for about 4 hours.

Nutritional facts: Calories 351, Carbs 6 g, Fat 23 g, Protein 36 g

Coconut Sesame Ginger Chicken

Ingredients:

Skinless, boneless chicken breasts – 1 ½ lbs.
Tomato puree – ½ cup
Apricot jam (unsweetened) – 1/3 cup
Chicken broth – 1/3 cup
Coconut aminos – 2 tablespoon
Sesame seed oil – 1 ½ tablespoon
Sweetener of choice – 1 tablespoon
Ground ginger – 1 teaspoon
Onion (minced) – ¼ cup
Red pepper flakes (crushed) – ½ teaspoon
Red bell pepper (chopped) – 2 tablespoon

Topping:
Sesame seeds – 2 teaspoon
Scallions (chopped) – 1 ½ tablespoon

Directions:-
1. Combine all the ingredients in a slow cooker and stir mix.
2. Cook for 4 hours on high.
3. Serve garnished with the sesame seeds and scallions.

Nutrition Information per serving: 220 Cal, 9 g total fat, 7 g net carbs, 3g fiber, 26 g protein.

Chilies Apple Cider Vinegar Chipotle Chicken

Ingredients:

Skinless, boneless chicken breasts – 1 ½ lbs.

Sauce:
Tomato sauce – 1/3 cup
Avocado oil – 2 tablespoon
Garlic cloves – 2
Mild green chilies (canned) – 2 tablespoon
Apple cider vinegar – 1 tablespoon
Lime juice – 3 tablespoon
Fresh cilantro – 1/3 cup
Sweetener of choice – 1 ½ teaspoon
Ground chipotle powder – 1 teaspoon
Sea salt - 1 teaspoon
Black pepper – ¼ teaspoon

Directions:

1. Place all the sauce ingredients in a blender and blend until smooth.
2. Arrange the chicken in the slow cooker and pour over the sauce.
3. Cook for 4-6 hours on high.

Nutrition Information per serving: 183 Cal, 9 g total fat, 2 g carbs, 0g fiber, 22 g protein.

Cream Cheese Tomato Chicken

Ingredients:

Frozen chicken breast (boneless) – 2 lbs.
Tomatoes (diced) – 1 ½ cups
Salsa – 16 oz.
Cream cheese – 8 oz.

Directions:

1. Place the chicken, tomatoes and salsa in a slow cooker.
2. Cook for 4-5 hours on high.
3. Add the cream cheese and cook for another 30 minutes.
4. Stir mix the chicken.
5. Serve on cauliflower rice.

Nutrition Information per serving: 349 Cal, 17.4 g total fat, 8 g carbs, 2.8 g fiber, 37.3 g protein.

Garlic Chicken Egg Dish

Ingredients:

Onions (chopped fine) – 2
Garlic clove (minced) – 1
Butter – ½ cup
Organic Ethiopian Berebere – 4 tablespoon
Whole Chicken (separated into legs, breasts and thighs) – 1
Celtic sea salt – 2 teaspoon
Organic hard boiled eggs (peeled) - 8

Directions:

1. Place the onions, garlic, butter, salt and Berebere in a slow cooker.
2. Cook for 8 hours on low.
3. Add the chicken and cook for another 8 hours on low.
4. Transfer the mixture into the serving dish and place in the eggs.

Nutrition Information per serving: 315 Cal, 22g total fat, 4 g carbs, 0.8 g fiber, 19 g protein.

Tasty BabyBack Ribs

Ingredients:

3 lb. baby back ribs, trimmed
1 Tbsp. paprika
1 Tbsp. garlic powder
½ onion, sliced
6 cloves garlic
½ c. water
2 c. sugar-free barbeque sauce

Directions:

1. Season ribs generously with paprika and garlic powder.
2. Place ribs in slow cooker with onion, garlic and water.
3. Cover and cook on high for 4 hours or low for 8 hours.
4. Preheat oven to 375ºF. Line a baking sheet with foil and spray with non-stick spray.
5. Using tongs, transfer ribs to baking sheet. Slather with barbeque sauce and bake for 10-15 minutes.

Nutritional facts:
Calories 525, Carbs 5 g, Fat 24 g, Protein 33 g

Bacon-Brussels Sprout Dip

Ingredients:

1 lb. Brussels sprouts, trimmed and quartered
2 Tbsp. extra virgin olive oil
2 cloves garlic, minced
Salt and pepper
4 oz. cream cheese
¼ c. sour cream
¼ c. mayonnaise
¾ c. mozzarella cheese, shredded
¼ c. Parmesan cheese, freshly grated
4 slices bacon, cooked and crumbled

Directions:

1. Preheat oven to 400ºF. Line a baking sheet with foil and spray with non-stick spray.
2. In a bowl, combine Brussels sprouts, olive oil, garlic, salt and pepper. Spread evenly on baking sheet and bake for 20-30 minutes.
3. Transfer Brussels sprout mixture to slow cooker with remaining ingredients. Mix thoroughly.
4. Cover and cook on low for 3 hours.

Nutritional facts:
Calories 406, Carbs 8 g, Fat 25 g, Protein 15 g

Garlic Lemon Cumin Ribs

Ingredients:

4 lb. pork ribs
2 Tbsp. garlic powder
2 Tbsp. sea salt
2 Tbsp. black pepper
1 Tbsp. cumin
3 lemons, juiced

Directions:

1. In a bowl, combine garlic powder, salt, pepper and cumin.
2. Rub spices over ribs, making sure to coat them thoroughly.
3. Arrange ribs in slow cooker, and pour lemon juice over ribs.
4. Cook on low for 8 hours or on high for 5 hours.

Nutritional facts:
Calories 287, Carbs 0.5 g, Fat 18 g, Protein 29 g

Butter Jalapeno Chicken

Ingredients:

Boneless chicken breasts - 2
Butter – 4 tablespoon
Sweet onion (chopped) – ½
Green bell pepper (chopped) - 1
Garlic cloves (minced) – 3
Jalapeno pepper (chopped) – 1
Salsa – 1 ½ cups
Cumin – ¼ teaspoon
Dried oregano – 1 teaspoon

Directions:

1. Melt the butter in a skillet and brown the chicken pieces in it. Transfer into a slow cooker.
2. Add the bell pepper, onion, jalapeno and garlic to the skillet and sauté for a while. Transfer into the slow cooker.
3. Mix the rest of the ingredients into the slow cooker.
4. Cook for 8 hours on low.

Nutrition Information per serving: 358 Cal, 25 g total fat, 15.75 g carbs, 4.75 g fiber, 35 g protein.

Thyme Spicy Drumsticks

Ingredients:

Chicken drumsticks (skinned) - 4
Bottled picante sauce – ½ cup
Bottled cayenne pepper sauce – 2 teaspoons
Smoked paprika – ½ teaspoon
Bay leaf – 1
Dried thyme – ¼ teaspoon
Olive oil – 2 teaspoon

Directions:

1. Place all the ingredients in a greased slow cooker.
2. Cook covered for 6 hours on low.

Nutrition facts: 209 Cal, 9 g total fat, 3 g carbs, 27 g protein.

Sweet & Sour Pork Ribs

Ingredients:

Country style pork ribs – 5 lbs.
Brown sugar substitute – ¾ cup
Soy sauce – ½ cup
Maple syrup (sugar-free) – ¼ cup
White vinegar – 1 tablespoon
Ketchup (sugar-free) – ½ cup
Salt – 1 teaspoon
Ground ginger – 1 teaspoon
Garlic cloves (minced) – 3
Red pepper flakes (crushed) – ½ teaspoon
Onion slices – 3
Sesame seeds – 1 tablespoon

Directions:

1. Whisk together all the ingredients in a bowl except the pork, onion and sesame seeds.
2. Layer the onion in a slow cooker and place the ribs over it.
3. Pour over the sauce and coat the ribs in it.
4. Cook covered for 6 hours on low.
5. Serve garnished with sesame seeds.

Nutrition Information per serving: 603 Cal, 34 g total fat, 9 g carb., 0 g fiber, 63 g protein.

Red Chilies Ginger Mandarin Chicken

Ingredients:

Chicken thighs – 6

Chinese Five spice powder – 1 tablespoon

Kosher salt – ½ teaspoon

Mandarin orange slices (no added sugar) – 1 cup

Garlic (minced) – 1 teaspoon

Ginger (minced – 1 tablespoon

Red chilies (sliced) – ½ teaspoon

Lime juice – 1 tablespoon

Granulated sugar substitute – 1 tablespoon

Sesame oil – 1 teaspoon

Fish sauce – 2 tablespoon

Xantham gum – ½ teaspoon

Directions:-
1. Season the chicken with salt and five spice powder and sear it in a pan on both sides.
2. Place the chicken in a slow cooker skin side up.
3. Mix together the rest of the ingredients except the gum and pour it over the chicken.
4. Cook covered for 6 hours on low.
5. Transfer the chicken into a platter.
6. Combine the sauce with the gum in a blender and blend for 20 seconds.
7. Pour over the chicken and serve.

Nutrition Information per serving: 392 Cal, 23 g total fat, 3.5 g net carbs, 37 g protein.

Yummy Garlic Cauliflower Pork

Ingredients:
Cauliflower Rice:
Cauliflower – 3 cups
Organic chicken broth – 2 tablespoon
Garlic powder – ¼ teaspoon
Sea salt – 1/8 teaspoon
Pork:
Pork butt roast (poke holes all over) – 3 lbs.
Hickory smoked and nitrate free bacon slices – 4
Hawaiian black lava sea salt – 1 ½ tablespoon
Garlic cloves (minced) – 5
Hickory liquid smoke – 2 tablespoon

Directions:
1. Place the bacon slices on the base of the slow cooker and spread the garlic on top.
2. Rub the salt over the roast and place it on the bacon, fat side down.
3. Pour the liquid smoke over and cook for 4-6 hours on high.
4. Cook another 2 hours on low.
5. Using forks, shred the meat and mix all the ingredients well.
6. Cook for another 30 minutes on low.
7. For the rice, microwave the cauliflower for 5 minutes and then combine the rice ingredients in a food processor, processing until riced.
8. Serve the pork with the rice.

Nutrition Information per serving: 182 Cal, 13 g total fat, 2 g carb., 0.9 g fiber, 14 g protein.

Oregano Paprika Pork Tenderloin

Ingredients :

1 1/2 lb pork tenderloin
2 Tbs smoked paprika
1/2 cup salsa of your choice
1 cup low sodium chicken broth or water
1 Tbsp oregano
Salt and pepper to taste

Directions:

1. In a bowl stir together the chicken stock, salsa, paprika, oregano, salt, and pepper.
2. Add the pork to your Slow Cooker.
3. Pour over the sauce and cook on HIGH for 4 hours.
4. Shred the pork with two forks and cook with the top off for an additional 20 minutes on HIGH.
5. Serve hot.

Nutrition Facts :

Carbs: 4.78g ,Fiber: 2,18g ,Protein: 29g ,Fat: 16g ,Calories: 388

Cinnamon Bacon Pork Loin

Ingredients:

4 lb. pork tenderloin
½ Granny Smith apple, thinly sliced
6 slices bacon
1 tsp. cinnamon

Directions:

1. In a pan, fry bacon until it is halfway done.
2. Make horizontal slices in pork loin, about ¾ of the way down (the loin should still be together in one piece).
3. Place apple slices in slits. Lay bacon on top of loin and sprinkle with cinnamon.
4. Place pork in slow cooker. Cover and cook on high for 3-4 hours or on low for 6-8 hours.

Nutritional Info Per Serving:
Calories 335, Carbs 13 g, Fat 8 g, Protein 48 g

Peanut Spicy Pork Sirloin

Ingredients:

2 Tbsp. coconut oil
4 lb. pork sirloin
Salt and pepper
3 tsp. ginger root, minced
3 cloves garlic
¼ c. natural peanut butter
½ c. tomato sauce
3 Tbsp. soy sauce
3 Tbsp. granulated sweetener, like Splenda
2 tsp. chili garlic paste
3 Tbsp. chicken stock

Directions:

1. In a large skillet, heat coconut oil over medium-high heat.
2. While skillet is heating, rub pork loin with salt, pepper and any other desired seasonings.
3. Sear pork for 2-3 minutes on each side, and remove to slow cooker.
4. In a food processor or high-speed blender, process remaining ingredients until smooth sauce forms. Pour sauce over pork, coating well.
5. Cover and cook on low for 3-4 hours.

Nutritional Info Per Serving:
Calories 392, Carbs 16 g, Fat 18 g, Protein 39 g

Ginger Chili Chicken

Ingredients:

Skinless chicken breasts (chopped) – 3
Jalapeno peppers (sliced) – 2
Chili pepper (chopped) – 1
Red bell pepper (chopped) – 1
Chicken broth – 8 oz.
Red pepper (crushed) – 1 tablespoon
Green onions (chopped) – ½ cup
Peanut butter – 6 teaspoon
Lemon juice – 4 teaspoon
Soy sauce – 4 teaspoon
Olive oil – 2 teaspoon
Ginger (ground) – 1 teaspoon
Garlic (minced) – 1 teaspoon
Fresh ground pepper – ½ teaspoon
Salt – to taste

Directions:

1. Combine all the ingredients in a bowl and marinate overnight in the refrigerator.
2. Transfer the ingredients into a slow cooker.
3. Cook covered for 6-8 hours on low.

Nutrition Information per serving: 150 Cal, 5.3 g total fat, , 4.9 g carbs, 1.3 g fiber, 20 g protein.

Basil Turkey Meatballs

Ingredients:

Frozen turkey meatballs – 1 (12 oz.) package
Bottled roasted red & yellow sweet peppers (drained, chopped) – ½ cup
Crushed red pepper – 1/8 teaspoon
Pasta sauce (reduced sodium) – 1 cup
Fresh basil (snipped) – for garnish

Directions:

1. Combine all the ingredients except the basil in a slow cooker.
2. Cook covered for 4-5 hours on low.
3. Stir gently and serve garnished with basil.

Nutrition Information per serving: 68 Cal, 4 g total fat (1 g sat. fat), 182 mg sodium, 3 g carbs, 6 g protein.

Weekend Beer Chicken

Ingredients:

Chicken breasts (boneless, skinless) – 1 ½ lbs.
Light beer – 1 (12 oz.) can
Salt – ½ teaspoon
Black pepper – ½ teaspoon
Red pepper flakes – ½ teaspoon
Dried oregano – ½ tablespoon

Directions:

1. Season the chicken with red pepper flakes, salt pepper and oregano and put into a slow cooker.
2. Pour the beer over the chicken.
3. Cook covered for 6-8 hours on low.
4. Shred the chicken using two forks.

Nutrition Information per serving: **139 Cal, 3 g total fat, 2 g carbs, 0 g fiber, 28 g protein.**

Turmeric Coconut Pork Curry

Ingredients:

2.2 pounds pork shoulder, cubed
1 Tablespoon coconut oil
1 yellow onion, diced
2 garlic cloves, minced
2 Tablespoons tomato paste
1 small can coconut milk – 12 fl ounces
1 cup water
½ cup white wine
1 teaspoon turmeric
1 teaspoon ginger powder
1 teaspoon curry powder
½ teaspoon paprika
Salt and pepper to taste

Directions:

1. In a pan, heat 1 tablespoon olive oil. Sauté the onion and garlic for 2-3 minutes.
2. Add the pork and brown it. Finish with tomato paste.
3. In the crock-pot, mix all remaining ingredients, submerge the meat in the liquid.
4. Cover, cook on low for 8 hours.

Nutritional values per serving: net Carb 7g; Protein 30g; Fat 24g , Carlories: 451

Serve with sour cream and cucumber cubes sprinkled with fresh chopped dill.

Black Olive Italian Chicken

Ingredients:

Chicken breasts (boneless, skinless) – 2 lbs.
Chicken broth (reduced-sodium) – 1 cup
Tomato paste – 3 tablespoon
Italian seasoning – 1 teaspoon
Salt and black pepper – to taste
Basil – ½ teaspoon
Red pepper flakes – ¼ teaspoon
Turkey pepperonis (halved) – 35
Black olives (reduced-sodium, sliced) – ½ cup

Directions:

1. Season the chicken with salt and pepper and place in a slow cooker.
2. Add in the olives and pepperoni.
3. Whisk together the rest of the ingredients and pour over the chicken.
4. Cook covered for 6 hours on low.
5. Shred the chicken using two forks.

Nutrition Information per serving: 307 Cal, 10 g total fat, 4 g carbs, 1 g fiber, 52 g protein.

CHAPTER 4 : SOUP & STEW RECIPES

Veggie Chicken Soup

Ingredients:

2.2 pounds chicken thighs, de-boned and cubed

1 cup chicken broth + 2 cups hot water

3 celery sticks, diced (approximately 1 ½ cups)

2 zucchini, diced

1 red bell pepper, diced

1 red onion, diced

2 garlic cloves, minced

1 bay leaf

1 teaspoon dried rosemary

Salt and pepper to taste

Directions:

1. Add all ingredients to the crock-pot.
2. Cover, cook on low for 6-8 hours.

Nutritional values per serving: net Carb 8g; Protein 37g; Fat 23g, Calories: 432

Serve with sour cream.

Special One-Pot Meal

Ingredients:

1 green bell pepper, chopped

1 cup fresh spinach

1 red onion, diced

2 garlic cloves, minced

1 regular can diced Italian tomatoes

2 cups chicken broth

2 Tablespoons tomato paste

1 cup black olives, sliced

1 cup dry white wine

2 bay leaves

1 teaspoon dry basil

¼ teaspoon crushed fennel seeds

1 ¾ cups medium-sized shrimp, peeled

1 ¾ cups cod, cubed

Salt and pepper to taste

Directions:

1. Add all ingredients (except the shrimp and cod) to the crock-pot.

2. Cover, cook on low 4.5 hours.

3. Add the shrimp and cod. Re-cover, cook on low for 30 minutes.

Nutritional values per serving: net Carb 9g; Protein 36g; Fat 25g, Calories: 436 Serve with nut bread and butter.

Ginger Pumpkin Soup

Ingredients:

Onion (diced) – 1

Ginger (crushed) – 1 teaspoon

Garlic (crushed) – 1 teaspoon

Butter – ½ stick

Pumpkin chunks – 1 lb.

Vegetable stock – 2 cups

Coconut cream – 1 2/3 cups

Salt and pepper – to taste

Directions:-
1. Combine all the ingredients in a slow cooker.
2. Cook for 4-6 hours on high.
3. Using an immersion blender puree the soup.

Nutrition Information per serving: 234 Cal, 21.7 g total fat, 11.4 g carb., 1.5g fiber, 2.3 g protein.

Cordon Bleu Chicken Soup

Ingredients:-

Ham (diced) – 12 oz.

Chicken breast – 1 lb.

Onion (diced) – 4 oz.

Mushrooms (chopped) – 5 oz.

Garlic (minced) – 3 tablespoon

Chicken broth – 6 cups

Tarragon – 2 teaspoon

Salted butter – 3 tablespoon

Sea salt – 1 teaspoon

Black pepper – 1 teaspoon

Heavy cream – 1 ½ cup

Sour cream – ½ cup

Parmesan cheese (grated) – ½ cup

Swiss cheese – 4 oz.

Directions:-

1. Combine the broth, mushroom, ham salt, pepper, tarragon and onion in the slow cooker on low and cook for a while.

2. Melt the butter in a pan and cook the garlic in it.

3. Add the chicken and sear it on all sides.

4. Transfer into a slow cooker along with the cheeses and cream.

5. Cook covered for 6 hours on low.

Nutrition Information per serving: 178 Cal, 12 g total fat, 2.75 g net carb., 16 g protein.

Minty-Ball Veggie Soup

Ingredients:

3 cups beef broth

1 medium zucchini, cut into sticks

2 celery sticks, diced (approximately 1 cup)

1 yellow onion, diced

5 garlic cloves, crushed

1 medium tomato, cubed

3 cups ground veal

½ cup Parmesan cheese

1 large egg

½ cup fresh mint, chopped

1 teaspoon dry oregano

1 teaspoon sweet paprika

Salt and pepper to taste

Directions:

1. Preheat crock-pot on low. Add broth, zucchini, celery, onion, tomato.

2. In a mixing bowl, combine meat, cheese, garlic, egg, mint, seasoning, salt and pepper. Mix well. Shape into mini-meatballs (approximately 45).

3. Heat olive oil in a pan, add meatballs. Brown for few minutes on all sides.

4. Add meatballs to the crock-pot. If necessary, add one cup hot water.

5. Cover, cook on low for 6-8 hours.

Nutritional values per serving: net Carb 11g; Protein 32g; Fat 25g, Calories: 395

Serve with nut bread and olives.

Sour Cream Beef Meatball Soup

Ingredients:

1 red bell pepper, diced

8-10 pearl onions, halved

2 garlic cloves, minced

2 Tablespoons olive oil

3 cups lean ground beef

1 egg

1 teaspoon dry savoury

Salt and pepper to taste

1 cup beef broth + 2 cups hot water

1 cup sour cream

Directions:

1. Preheat crock-pot on low. Add vegetables and olive oil.

2. In a bowl, combine meat, egg, dry savoury, salt and pepper. Mix well and shape into bite-size meatballs (approximately 30).

3. In a pot, boil the broth, add the meatballs and heat for 2 minutes.

4. Add the meatballs, and broth to the crock-pot. If necessary, add ½ cup hot water.

5. Cover, cook on low for 6 hours.

6. Open the lid and ladle out a small amount of liquid, cool it slightly and use to thin the sour cream. Add salt and pepper, if needed, and return the cream mixture to the pot.

7. Stir gently, not to break the meatballs. Serve hot.

Nutritional values per serving: net Carb 11g; Protein 27g; Fat 28g, Calories: 409

Serve with basil-olive paste on nut crackers.

Heavy Cream Corned Beef Soup

Ingredients:

Onion (diced) – 1

Celery ribs (diced) – 2

Garlic cloves (minced) – 2

Butter – 3 tablespoon

Corned beef (chopped) – 1 lb.

Beef stock – 4 cups

Sauerkraut – 1 cup

Sea salt – 1 teaspoon

Caraway seeds – 1 teaspoon

Black pepper – ¾ teaspoon

Heavy cream – 2 cups

Swiss cheese (shredded) – 1 ½ cup

Directions:

1. Heat the pan and sauté the onion, garlic, celery and butter in it.

2. Transfer the mixture into the slow cooker.

3. Place the rest of the ingredients except the cheese and cream in the slow cooker.

4. Cook for 4 ½ hours on low.

5. Mix in the cheese and cream and cook for another hour.

Nutrition Information per serving: 225 Cal, 18.5 g total fat, 4 g net carb., 11.5 g protein.

Sausage Lentil Soup

Ingredients:

Italian sausage – 1 ½ lbs.

Butter – 2 tablespoon

Olive oil – 2 tablespoon

Chicken stock – 5 cups

Lentils (rinsed) – 1 ½ cups

Spinach – 1 cup

Carrots (diced) – ½ cup

Garlic cloves (minced) – 4

Leek (cleaned, trimmed) – 1

Celery rib (diced) - 1

Heavy cream – 1 cup

Parmesan cheese (shredded) – ½ cup

Dijon mustard – 2 tablespoon

Red wine vinegar – 2 tablespoon

Sea salt and black pepper – to taste

Directions:

1. Place the lentils and stock in the slow cooker.

2. Heat butter and olive oil in a saucepan and brown the sausage in it.

3. Transfer the sausage into the slow cooker and sauté the carrots, onions, spinach, leek, garlic, salt, pepper and celery in the drippings left behind for 10 minutes.

4. Transfer the mixture into the slow cooker with the rest of the ingredients.

5. Cook for 6-8 hours on low.

Nutrition Information per serving: 195 Cal, 14 g total fat, 4.9 g net carb., 11 g protein.

Spearmint Lamb Heart and Liver Soup

Ingredients:

3 cups lamb hearts and livers, well washed

1 cup lamb meat, cubed

2 cups broth, your choice

2 cups hot water

2 bunches spring onions, diced

1 bunch fresh spearmint, chopped

2 cups fresh spinach

1 teaspoon garlic powder

1 teaspoon dry basil

1 teaspoon sweet paprika

1 teaspoon ground pimento

4 cloves, lightly crushed

½ teaspoon cinnamon

4 Tablespoons of olive oil

Salt and pepper to taste

1 egg

1 cup full-fat Greek yogurt

Directions:

1. Add all ingredients to the crock-pot, except the egg and yogurt.

2. Cover, cook on low for 10 hours.

3. Take out the meaty pieces and into small, bite size pieces. Return to crock-pot.

4. Beat the egg and yogurt together slowly. Ladle in some of the cooked liquid. Stir slowly to combine.

5. Return the mixture to crock-pot. Stir well to combine. Serve.

Nutritional values per serving: net Carb 12g; Protein 56g; Fat38g, Calories: 560

Serve with nut bread and butter.

Coriander Cinnamon Broccolic Oxtail Pot

Ingredients:

3 pounds oxtail, cut into 1 inch pieces (ask your butcher to cut)

2 Tablespoons olive oil

1 red onion, diced

3 garlic cloves, minced

3 inch piece fresh ginger, peeled, thinly sliced

1 regular can Italian diced tomatoes

1 teaspoon ground cardamom

1 teaspoon ground cumin

1 teaspoon ground coriander seeds

½ teaspoon cinnamon

1 ½ teaspoon salt

1 teaspoon fresh ground black pepper

1 cup beef broth + 1 cup hot water

5 small turnips, cubed

1 head of broccoli, chopped

1 cup mushrooms, washed, dried, diced into small pieces

Directions:

1. Preheat crock-pot on low.

2. In a pan, heat the olive oil. Brown the oxtail on all sides. Transfer to the crock-pot.

3. In the same pan, sauté the onions for 5 minutes, once they are translucent, add the garlic and ginger, heat for 1 minute.

4. Pour the onion, garlic, ginger mixture over the oxtail.

5. Add the remaining ingredients to the same browning pan, bring to a boil.

6. Once hot, pour the sauce in the crock-pot, stir well. The liquid should cover everything. If necessary, add ½ cup hot water.

7. Cover, cook on low for 8-10 hours.

Nutritional values per serving: net Carb 14g; Protein 68g; Fat 31g , Calories: 510

Serve with nut bread and butter.

Spicy Chorizo Chicken Soup

Ingredients:

Boneless, skinless chicken thighs – 4 lbs.

Chorizo – 1 lb.

Chicken stock – 4 cups

Heavy cream – 1 cup

Stewed tomatoes – 1 can

Minced garlic – 2 tablespoon

Worcestershire sauce – 2 tablespoon

Frank's red hot sauce – 2 tablespoon

Sour cream and parmesan for garnish

Directions:-

1. Heat a skillet and brown the sausage in it.
2. Place the chicken in the slow cooker and then add in the rest of the ingredients including the chorizo.
3. Cook for 3 hours on high.
4. Break the thighs apart and cook for another 30 minutes.
5. Garnish with the cream and Parmesan.

Nutrition Information per serving: 659 Cal, 37 g total fat, 6 g carb., 1 g fiber, 52 g protein.

Thyme Garlic Bacon Chicken Chili Soup

Ingredients:

Unsalted butter – 2 tablespoons

Onion (chopped) – 1

Pepper (chopped) – 1

Chicken thighs – 8

Bacon slices – 8

Thyme – 1 tablespoon

Salt – 1 teaspoon

Pepper – 1 teaspoon

Garlic (minced) – 1 tablespoon

Coconut flour – 1 tablespoon

Lemon juice – 3 tablespoon

Chicken stock – 1 cup

Coconut milk (unsweetened) – ¼ cup

Tomato paste – 3 tablespoons

Directions:

1. Add the butter to the slow cooker and spread the onion and peppers in it.
2. Place the chicken thighs on top and then layer the bacon.
3. Add the rest of the ingredients.
4. Cook for 6 hours on low.
5. Break the thighs apart prior to serving.

Nutrition Information per serving: 396 Cal, 21 g total fat, 7 g carb., 2 g fiber, 41 g protein.

Cauliflower Ham Stew

Ingredients:-

Leftover ham (diced) – 3 cups

Frozen cauliflower florets – 16 oz.

Heavy cream – ¼ cup

Chicken broth – 14.5 oz.

Salt – ¼ teaspoon

Garlic cloves – 4

Cheddar cheese (grated) – 8 oz.

Garlic powder – ½ teaspoon

Onion powder – ½ teaspoon

Dash of pepper

Directions:-

1. Combine all the ingredients in a slow cooker.
2. Cook for 4 hours on high.

Nutrition Information per serving: 320 Cal, 20.6 g total fat, 7.5 g carb., 3 g fiber, 23.3 g protein.

Spicy Onion Turkey

Ingredients:

Ground turkey (cooked) – 1 lb.

Sweet yellow onion (diced) – ½ cup

Jalapeno pepper (sliced) – 1

Pureed tomatoes – 1 (28 oz.) can

Serrano chilies (sliced) – 2

Chili powder – 2 tablespoon

Vinegar – 1 tablespoon

Sea salt (coarse) – 1 teaspoon

Directions:

1. Combine all the ingredients in a slow cooker.
2. Cook covered for 3-6 hours on low.

Nutrition Information per serving: 111 Cal, 7 g total fat, 4 g carb., 1 g fiber, 8 g protein.

Chilli Turkey Soup

Ingredients:

2.2 pounds ground turkey

2 Tablespoons butter

1 red onion, diced

2 garlic cloves, minced

1 cup celery, diced

1 teaspoon chilli powder

1 teaspoon dry oregano

1 teaspoon dry thyme

1 teaspoon of dry basil

1 teaspoon of ground cumin

2 regular cans Italian diced tomatoes

14 fl ounce jar tomato passata

1 cup chicken broth

Salt and pepper to taste

Directions:

1. In a pan, melt the butter. Add the diced onion, sauté for 2 minutes then add the ground turkey, cook thoroughly.

2. Add the vegetables and spices. Stir and cook the mixture for an additional 2 minutes.

3. Transfer the mixture to the crock-pot.

4. Pour the tomatoes and broth over the mixture and stir.

5. Cover, cook on low for 6 hours.

Nutritional values per serving: net Carb 10g; Protein 32g; Fat 19g , Calories: 310

Serve with avocado slices and fried, crumbled bacon.

Spicy Rabbit Stew

Ingredients:

1 rabbit, in portion size pieces

2 cups spicy Spanish sausage, cut in chunks

2 Tablespoons butter, divided

1 red onion, sliced

1 cup button mushrooms, washed and dried

1 teaspoon cayenne pepper

1 teaspoon sweet paprika

1 teaspoon salt

1 teaspoon fresh ground black pepper

1 cup chicken broth+1 cup hot water

Directions:

1. Butter the crock-pot.

2. In a large pan, melt the butter, add the pieces of rabbit, brown on all sides. Transfer to crock-pot.

3. In the same pan, sauté the onions, sausage chunks, and spices for 2-3 minutes. Pour in chicken broth to deglaze the pan, heat on high for 1 minute then pour the mixture over the rabbit.

4. Add the mushrooms. Adjust the seasoning, if needed.

5. Add the water. Cover, cook on high for 6 hours. Serve.

Nutritional values per serving: net Carb 12g; Protein 44g; Fat 28g, Calories: 389

Serve with tomato slices, with olive oil and fresh, chopped parsley.

Delicious Chili Pork Stew

Ingredients:

Pork shoulder (cooked, sliced, chopped) - 1 lb.

Cumin – 2 teaspoon

Garlic (minced) – 1 teaspoon

Salt – ½ teaspoon

Pepper – ½ teaspoon

Chili powder – 2 teaspoon

Paprika – 1 teaspoon

Oregano – 1 teaspoon

Cinnamon – ¼ teaspoon

Bay leafs – 2

Button mushrooms (chopped) – 6 oz.

Jalapeno (sliced) – ½

Onion (sliced) – ½

Green bell pepper (sliced) – ½

Red bell pepper (sliced) – ½

Lime (juiced) – ½

Strong coffee – ½ cup

Gelatinous bone broth – 2 cups

Chicken broth – 2 cups

Tomato paste – ¼ cup

Olive oil – 2 tablespoon

Directions:

1. Heat oil in a skillet and sauté the veggies in it for a couple of minutes.
2. Combine all the ingredients in a slow cooker include the sautéed veggies.
3. Cook covered for 4-10 hours on low.

Nutrition Information per serving: 386 Cal, 28.9 g total fat, 6.4 g net carb., 19.9 g protein.

Thyme Celery Bacon Chowder

Ingredients:

Thick cut bacon – 13 slices

Onion (chopped) – 1 cup

Celery (chopped) – 1 cup

Whole baby clams (with juice) – 2 cans

Chicken Broth – 2 cups

Heavy whipping cream – 2 cups

Pepper – 1 teaspoon

Salt – 1 teaspoon

Ground thyme – 1 teaspoon

Directions:

1. Cook the bacon in a skillet until crispy. Remove and once cooled crumble it.

2. Sauté the celery and onion in the bacon grease and transfer into the slow cooker.

3. Combine the rest of ingredients in a slow cooker.

4. Cook covered for 4-6 hours on low.

Nutrition facts: 427 Cal, 30 g total fat, 0 g fiber, 27 g protein.

Almond Curried Chicken Stew

Ingredients :

8 bone-in chicken thighs

2 tbsp. olive oil or coconut oil

6 carrots, cut in 2-inch pieces

1 sweet onion, cut in thin wedges

1 cup unsweetened coconut milk

1/4 cup mild (or hot) curry paste

Toasted almonds, coriander and fresh green or red chili

Directions:

1. Cook chicken in a pan skin side down, in hot olive oil for 8 minutes, or until browned.

2. Remove from heat; drain and discard fat.

3. In a slow cooker combine carrots and onion.

4. Whisk together half the coconut milk and the curry paste; pour over carrots and onion

5. Place chicken, skin side up on top of vegetables, pour over olive oil from pan.

6. Cover and cook on high for 3.5 to 4 hours or on low for 7 to 8 hours.

7. Remove chicken from slow cooker. Skim off excess fat from sauce in cooker, then stir in remaining coconut milk.

8. Serve stew in bowls. Top each serving with toasted almonds, coriander, fresh chili and a dollop of yoghurt or crème fraiche.

Nutrition Facts : Calories 321 ,Carbs 20g ,Protein 14g ,Fats 22g

Cumin Chili Beef Tomato Bacon

Ingredients:

Ground beef – 2 lbs.

Bacon – 6 slices

Kielbasa – 8 oz.

Onion (chopped) – 1/2

Black coffee – 1 cup

Beef Broth – 1 cup

Whole tomatoes – 2 cans

Butter – 2 tablespoons

Worcestershire sauce – 2 tablespoons

Cocoa powder – 1 tablespoon

Chili powder – 1 tablespoon

Cumin – 1 teaspoon

Paprika – 2 teaspoon

Garlic powder – 2 teaspoon

Salt and pepper – to taste

Liquid stevia – 10 drops

Directions:

1. Puree the tomatoes in a food processor and place it in a crock pot.

2. Heat a skillet and brown the beef in it. Transfer into a bowl.

3. Melt the butter in the pan and sauté the onions in it. Add in the bacon and kielbasa, cooking until the bacon is crispy.

4. Mix in the ground beef and garlic powder and cook for another 5 minutes.

5. Transfer the meat mixture into the slow cooker along with the rest of the ingredients and mix well.

6. Cook covered for 4 hours on high.

7. Transfer the slow cooker contents into a pot and cook for 45 minutes on medium flame.

Nutrition Information per serving: 465 Cal, 30 g total fat, 124 mg chol., 936 mg sodium, 9 g carb., 4 g fiber, 38 g protein.

Simple Seafood Stew

Ingredients:

1 tablespoon olive oil

2 onions, diced

4 stalks celery, chopped

4 garlic cloves, minced

1 teaspoon dried oregano

½ teaspoon ground black pepper

1 tablespoon tomato paste

1 tablespoon flour

3 cups chicken stock

1 can tomato, onion and chili mix

1 -2 cup tomato cocktail juice

4 chicken breasts, cut into bite size pieces

2 packets mixed frozen seafood, you can add extra mussels in at the end

2 peppers (red and green)

1 jalapeno pepper, chopped

¼ cup parsley, chopped

1 teaspoon chili powder

1 pinch cayenne pepper

1 tbsp. butter

Directions :

1. In a large pan heat the olive oil and fry onions and celery

2. Add garlic, oregano, peppercorns.

3. Stir in tomato paste and almond flour and cook another minute.

4. Add chicken stock, tomatoes and tomato juice and bring to a boil. Continue to cook for about 3-5 more minutes. Remove from heat and transfer mixture to slow cooker.

5. Add chicken and stir to combine. Cover and cook on high for 3 hours or low for 6 hours.

6. Stir in mixed bags of frozen and parsley.

7. Cover and cook on high for 30 minutes

Nutrition Facts :

Calories 177

Carbs 15g

Protein 21g

Fats 7g

Mustard Sausage Lentil Soup

Ingredients:

Italian sausage – 1 ½ lbs.

Butter – 2 tablespoon

Olive oil – 2 tablespoon

Chicken stock – 5 cups

Lentils (rinsed) – 1 ½ cups

Spinach – 1 cup

Carrots (diced) – ½ cup

Garlic cloves (minced) – 4

Leek (cleaned, trimmed) – 1

Celery rib (diced) - 1

Heavy cream – 1 cup

Parmesan cheese (shredded) – ½ cup

Dijon mustard – 2 tablespoon

Red wine vinegar – 2 tablespoon

Sea salt and black pepper – to taste

Directions:

1. Place the lentils and stock in the slow cooker.

2. Heat butter and olive oil in a saucepan and brown the sausage in it.

3. Transfer the sausage into the slow cooker and sauté the carrots, onions, spinach, leek, garlic, salt, pepper and celery in the drippings left behind for 10 minutes.

4. Transfer the mixture into the slow cooker with the rest of the ingredients.

5. Cook for 6-8 hours on low.

Nutrition Information : 195 Cal, 14 g total fat, 4.9 g net carb., 11 g protein.

Delicious Mushroom Chicken Soup

Ingredients:

Ham (diced) – 12 oz.

Chicken breast – 1 lb.

Onion (diced) – 4 oz.

Mushrooms (chopped) – 5 oz.

Garlic (minced) – 3 tablespoon

Chicken broth – 6 cups

Tarragon – 2 teaspoon

Salted butter – 3 tablespoon

Sea salt – 1 teaspoon

Black pepper – 1 teaspoon

Heavy cream – 1 ½ cup

Sour cream – ½ cup

Parmesan cheese (grated) – ½ cup

Swiss cheese – 4 oz.

Directions:

1. Combine the broth, mushroom, ham salt, pepper, tarragon and onion in the slow cooker on low and cook for a while.

2. Melt the butter in a pan and cook the garlic in it.

3. Add the chicken and sear it on all sides.

4. Transfer into a slow cooker along with the cheeses and cream.

5. Cook covered for 6 hours on low.

Nutrition Information : 178 Cal, 12 g total fat, 2.75 g net carb., 16 g protein.

Yello Onion Creamy Chicken Soup

Ingredients:

Skinless, boneless chicken breasts (cooked, shredded) – 4 cups

Ranch dressing – 4 tablespoon

Celery stalks (chopped) – 2

Yellow onion (chopped) – ¼ cup

Cream cheese – 8 oz.

Salted butter – 6 tablespoon

Chicken broth – 8 cups

Bacon – 7 slices

Directions:
1. Cook the bacon in a pan until crispy and then crumble it.
2. Add all the ingredients to the slow cooker.
3. Cook covered for 4 hours on low.

Nutrition facts: 444 Cal, 34 g total fat, , 1 g fiber, 28 g protein.

Shallot Mushroom Chowder

Ingredients:

Cremini mushrooms (sliced) – 6 oz.

Chicken breasts – 1 lb.

Garlic cloves (minced) – 4

Shallot (chopped) – 1

Leek (sliced) – 1

Celery ribs (diced) – 2

Sweet onion (thinly sliced) – 1

Butter – 4 tablespoon

Chicken stock – 2 cups

Cream cheese – 8 oz.

Heavy cream – 1 cup

Bacon (cooked, crumbled) – 1 lb.

Sea salt – 1 teaspoon

Black pepper – 1 teaspoon

Garlic powder – 1 teaspoon

Dried thyme – 1 teaspoon

Directions:

1. Combine the leek, garlic, shallots, celery, onions, mushrooms, 1 cup chicken stock, salt, pepper and 2 tablespoon butter in a slow cooker and cook covered for 1 hours on low.

2. Melt the remaining butter in a skillet and sear the chicken breasts in it. Chop into cubes.

3. Remove the chicken and deglaze the skillet using the chicken stock.

4. Add the chicken along with the chicken stock to the slow cooker.

5. Stir in the rest of the ingredients.

6. Cook covered for 6-8 hours on low.

Nutrition facts: 355 Cal, 28 g total fat, 4.4 g carb., 0.62 g fiber, 21 g protein.

Creamy Thyme Chicken Stew

Ingredients:

Chicken thighs (skinless, deboned, diced) – 28 oz.

Chicken stock – 2 cups

Celery ribs (chopped) – 2

Carrots (peeled, chopped finely) - 2

Onion (chopped) – ½

Dried rosemary – ½ teaspoon

Dried thyme – ¼ teaspoon

Dried oregano – ½ teaspoon

Garlic cloves (minced) – 3

Spinach – 1 cup

Heavy cream – ½ cup

Salt and pepper – to taste

Xantham gum – 1/8 teaspoon

Directions:

1. Combine the chicken, celery, onion, chicken, carrots, garlic, and herbs in a slow cooker.
2. Cook covered for 4 hours on low.
3. Season with salt and pepper and mix in the cream and spinach.
4. Whisk in the xantham gum and cook for 10 minutes.

Nutrition facts: 228 Cal, 11 g total fat, 5g carb., 23 g protein.

Chili Bell Pepper Sausage Beef

Ingredients:

Ground beef – 1 lb.

Ground hot Italian sausage – 1 lb.

Green bell pepper (diced) – ½ cup

Yellow onion (chopped) – ½

Diced tomatoes in tomato juice – 1 can

Tomato paste – 6 oz.

Chili powder – 1 tablespoon

Ground cumin – ½ tablespoon

Bay leaves - 2

Garlic cloves (minced) – 3

Water – 1/3 cup

Directions:

1. Brown the beef and sausage in a skillet and then transfer into a slow cooker.
2. Add the rest of the ingredients to the slow cooker.
3. Cook covered for 6-8 hours on low.

Nutrition facts: 387 Cal, 24 g total fat, 7.2 g net carb., 33.5 g protein.

Nutritious Buffalo Chicken Soup

Ingredients:

Chicken breast (cubed) – 1 lb.

Chicken stock – 32 oz.

Buffalo wing sauce – ½ cup

Green onions (chopped) – 4

Carrots (chopped) – 2

Celery ribs (diced) – 2

Garlic cloves (minced) – 2

Sharp Cheddar cheese (shredded) – 1 cup

Parmesan cheese (shredded) – 2/3 cup

Blue cheese (crumbled) – ¼ cup

Italian flat leaf parsley (chopped) – 2 tablespoon

Directions:

1. Combine all the ingredients in a slow cooker except the cheeses and parsley.
2. Cook covered for 6 hours on low.
3. Mix in the cheeses.
4. Cook covered for another hour.
5. Garnish with parsley.

Nutrition facts: 146 Cal, 5 g total fat, 2 g net carb., 13 g protein.

Sweet Potato Sausage Soup

Ingredients:

Hot Italian sausage (casings discarded) – 1 lb.

Onion (diced) – 1

Olive oil – 2 tablespoons

Sweet potato (cubed) – 1 lb.

Garlic (minced) – 2 tablespoon

Cremini mushrooms (quartered) – 6 oz.

Chicken stock – 6 cups

Fresh baby spinach leaves – 6 oz.

Black pepper – 1 teaspoon

Garlic salt – 1 tablespoon

Directions:

1. Heat oil in a pan and sauté the onions and garlic in it.
2. Add the sausage and cook until browned.
3. Transfer into a slow cooker and mix in the rest of the ingredients except the spinach.
4. Cook covered for 6 hours on low.
5. Mix in the spinach and cook for another 30 minutes.

Nutrition facts: 138 Cal, 9 g total fat, 5.5 g net carb., 6.5 g protein.

Buttery Red Pepper Soup

Ingredients:

Fire roasted tomatoes – 2 (14.5 oz.) cans

Roasted red peppers – 12 oz. jar

Chicken stock – 3 cups

Tomato paste – 2 tablespoon

Dried basil – 2 teaspoon

Sea salt – 1 ½ teaspoon

Dried oregano – 1 teaspoon

Black pepper – ½ teaspoon

Onion (diced) – 1

Garlic cloves (minced) – 3

Butter – 3 tablespoon

Heavy cream – ½ cup

Smoked Gouda cheese (shredded) – 8 oz.

Directions:

1. Melt butter in a skillet and sauté the onion and garlic in it.

2. Transfer the mixture into the slow cooker along with the rest of the ingredients except the cheese and cream.

3. Cook covered for 4 hours on low.

4. Puree the soup using an immersion blender.

5. Stir in the cream and cheese and cook for another hour covered.

Nutrition Information per serving: 158 Cal, 10 g total fat, 5 g net carb., 6 g protein.

CHAPTER 5: LAMB & BEEF RECIPES

Shoulder Beef in BBQ Sauce

Ingredients:

8 pounds beef shoulder, whole

1 Tablespoon butter

1 yellow onion, diced

1 garlic bulb, peeled and minced

4 Tablespoons red wine vinegar

2 Tablespoons Worcestershire sauce

4 Tablespoons Swerve (or suitable substitute)

1 Tablespoon mustard

1 teaspoon salt

1 teaspoon fresh ground black pepper

Directions:

1. In a bowl, mix seasoning together. Set aside.

2. In a pan, melt the butter, add the meat. Brown on all sides. Transfer to crock-pot. In the same pan, fry the onion for 2-3 minutes, pour over the meat.

4. Pour in the seasoning. Cover, cook on low for 10 hours.

6. Remove from crock-pot, place on a platter, cover with foil, let it rest for 1 hour.

7. Turn the crock pot on high, reduce the remaining liquid by half and serve with the shredded beef.

Nutritional facts: net Carb 4g; Protein 75g; Fat 22g, Calories: 310

Malaysian Beef Curry

Ingredients:

Stewing beef (cubed) – 21.1 oz.

Coconut cream – 1 cup

Red onion (quartered) – 1

Ground cardamom – 1 teaspoon

Ground coriander – 2 teaspoon

Turmeric powder – 1 teaspoon

Chinese five spice – 1 teaspoon

Chili powder – ½ teaspoon

Ground cumin – 1 teaspoon

Ground cinnamon – 1 teaspoon

Leafy greens – a handful

Directions:

1. Combine all the ingredients in the slow cooker except the leafy greens and stir well.
2. Cook for 4-6 hours on high.
3. 5 minutes prior to completion of cook time, mix in the leafy greens.

Nutrition Information per serving: 256 Cal, 14.1 g total fat, 2 g carb., 0.9 g fiber, 29.1 g protein.

Rosemary Beef Brisket

Ingredients:

6.6 pounds beef brisket, whole

2 Tablespoons olive oil

2 Tablespoons apple cider vinegar

1 teaspoon dry oregano

1 teaspoon dry thyme

1 teaspoon dried rosemary

2 Tablespoons paprika

1 teaspoon Cayenne pepper

1 tablespoon salt

1 teaspoon fresh ground black pepper

Directions:

1. In a bowl, mix dry seasoning, add olive oil, apple cider vinegar.

2. Place the meat in the crock-pot, generously coat with seasoning mix.

3. Cover, cook on low for 12 hours.

4. Remove the brisket from the liquid, place on a pan. Sear it under the broiler for 2-4 minutes, watch it carefully so the meat doesn't burn.

5. Cover the meat with foil, let it rest for 1 hour. Slice and serve.

Nutritional facts: net Carb 1g; Protein 70g; Fat 28g, Calories: 410

Onion Cumin Beef And Cabbage Roast

Ingredients:

1 red onion, quartered

2 garlic cloves, minced

2-3 stocks celery, diced (approximately 1 cup)

4-6 dry pimento berries

2 bay leaves

5.5 pounds beef brisket (two pieces)

1 teaspoon chilli powder

1 teaspoon ground cumin

2 cups broth, beef + 2 cups hot water

Salt and pepper to taste

1 medium cabbage (approximately 2.2 pounds), cut in half, then quartered

Directions:

1. Add all ingredients, except cabbage, to crock-pot in order of list.

2. Cover, cook on low for 7 hours.

3. Uncover, add the cabbage on top of the stew.

4. Re-cover, cook for 1 additional hour.

Nutritional facts: net Carb 8g; Protein 32g; Fat 25g, Calories : 399

Serve with nut bread slices and mayonnaise.

Garlic Juicy Beef Pot Roast

Ingredients:

Beef arm roast (excess fat trimmed) – 2 lbs.

Kosher sea salt – 1 ½ teaspoons

Ground black pepper – ¾ teaspoon

Fresh basil (finely chopped) – ¾ teaspoon

Yellow onion (finely chopped) – ½ cup

Garlic cloves (minced) – 4

Bay leaves – 2

Beef stock – 2 cups

Directions:
1. Season all sides of the roast with basil, salt and pepper.
2. Put in the slow cooker and add in the rest of the ingredients.
3. Cook for 8-10 hours on low.
4. Discard the bay leaves and slice the roast.

Nutrition facts: 234 Cal, 10.3 g total fat, , 1 g fiber, 33.1 g protein.

Broccoli Sesame Coconut Beef

Ingredients:

Beef chuck roast (boneless, sliced into thin strips) – 1 lb.

Organic beef bone broth – 1 cup

Coconut aminos – ½ cup

Sesame oil – 1 tablespoon

Garlic cloves (minced) – 3

Ginger (grated) – 1 tablespoon

Guar gum – ½ teaspoon

Celtic sea salt and pepper – to taste

Organic broccoli florets (frozen) – 1 cup

Directions:

1. Mix together the broth, sweetener, coconut aminos, ginger, garlic and sesame oil and add it to the slow cooker.
2. Place the sliced beef in it and toss.
3. Cook for 4-6 hours on low.
4. Whisk together the guar gum and some cooking liquid and add it to the slow cooker.
5. Season with salt and pepper and cook for 30 minutes more.
6. Mix in the broccoli.

Nutrition facts: 281 Cal, 11 g total fat, 4 g carb., 1.5 g fiber, 37.9 g protein.

Slow Cooking Balsamic Roast Beef

Ingredients:

3 lb. boneless chuck roast

½ c. balsamic vinegar

1 c. beef broth

1 Tbsp. soy sauce

1 Tbsp. Worcestershire sauce

A pinch of granulated sweetener, like Splenda

½ tsp. cayenne pepper

4 cloves garlic, roughly chopped

Directions:

1. Place chuck roast in slow cooker.
2. In a bowl, combine remaining ingredients. Pour over chuck roast.
3. Cover and cook on high for 4 hours or low for 8 hours.
4. Remove beef from slow cooker and shred with 2 forks. Place in serving dish and pour about ½ cup of gravy on top.

Nutritional Info Per Serving:

Calories 362, Carbs 9 g, Fat 14 g, Protein 47 g

Coconut Burgundy Beef

Ingredients:

2 Tbsp. coconut oil

2 lb. beef steak top round, trimmed and cubed

Salt and pepper

¼ c. water

4 slices bacon, cooked and cut into 1" pieces

½ onion, sliced

2 cloves garlic, minced

½ tsp. dried marjoram leaves

½ c. dry red wine

½ c. beef broth

½ oz. dried porcini mushrooms, ground

1 Tbsp. extra virgin olive oil

8 oz. crimini mushrooms, sliced

Directions:

1. In a large skillet, melt coconut oil over medium-high heat. Season beef cubes with salt and pepper, and sear until browned on the outside. Remove beef to slow cooker.

2. Add water to skillet, scraping up any brown bits sticking to the pan.

3. Pour skillet juices, bacon, onion and garlic into slow cooker.

4. In a bowl, whisk together marjoram leaves, wine, broth and dried porcini mushrooms. Add mixture to slow cooker and season with salt and pepper.

5. Cover and cook on low for 6-8 hours.

6. Just before serving, sauté crimini mushrooms in olive oil. Mix into beef stew and serve.

Nutritional Info Per Serving:

Calories 524, Carbs 5 g, Fat 26 g, Protein 58 g

Green Beans Garlic Minty Lamb

Ingredients:

Lamb leg (bone-in) – 1

Ghee – 2 tablespoon

Garlic cloves - 4

Mint (chopped) – ¼ cup

Green beans (trimmed) – 6 cups

Salt – ½ teaspoon

Ground black pepper – to taste

Directions:
1. Season the lamb with salt and pepper.
2. Heat the ghee in a pot and sear the lamb on all sides.
3. Transfer the lamb into the slow cooker and add the garlic and mint to it.
4. Cook covered for 4 hours on high.
5. Transfer the lamb onto a platter and add the green beans to the slow cooker.
6. Cook for 2 hours.
7. Serve the lamb with the green beans.

Nutrition facts: 524 Cal, 28.4 g total fat, 4.4 g fiber, 35.3 g protein.

Mushroom Beef Stroganoff

Ingredients:

Brown onion (sliced, quartered) – 1

Garlic cloves (crushed) – 2

Streaky bacon slices (diced) - 2

Stewing steak beef (cubed) – 1 lb.

Smoked paprika – 1 teaspoon

Tomato paste – ¼ cup

Beef stock – 1 cup

Mushrooms (quartered) – 9 oz.

Directions:

1. Combine all the ingredients in the slow cooker.
2. Cook for 4-6 hours on high.

Nutrition facts: 260 Cal, 14.2 g total fat, 6 g carb., 1.2 g fiber, 26.5 g protein.

Mouth-watering Spicy Shredded Beef

Ingredients:

Boned beef chuck – 2 ½ pounds

Chopped tomatoes – 1 (14 ½ oz.) can

Chipotle sauce – 1 (7 oz.) can

Drained jalapenos chiles (diced) - 1 (4 oz.) can

Chopped onion – 1

Minced garlic cloves – 3

Chili powder – 2 tablespoons

Honey – 1 tablespoon

Kosher salt – 2 ½ teaspoons

Ground cumin – 1 teaspoon

Beef broth – 2 cups

Directions:

1. Combine all the ingredients in a slow cooker.
2. Cook covered for 8-10 hours on low, until beef is tender.
3. During the last ½ hour of cooking, cook uncovered to thicken the sauce.
4. Remove the meat, shred the meat using forks and return it to the cooker.

Nutrition facts: 261 Cal, 11 g total, 1.8g fiber, 30 g protein.

Chili Spiced Beef Eye Roast

Ingredients:

Lean ground beef eye roast – 3 lbs.

Worcestershire sauce – 2 tablespoon

Fresh lime juice – 4 tablespoon

Onion (diced) – 1 ½ cups

Red bell pepper (diced) – 1 cup

Garlic cloves (minced) – 3

Serrano chilies (seeded, minced) – 3

Salt and pepper – to taste

Beef broth (non-fat) – ½ cup

Canned diced tomatoes – 1 cup

Dried oregano – ½ teaspoon

Directions:

1. Season the beef roast with salt and pepper and put it in the slow cooker.
2. Whisk the rest of the ingredients together and pour over the beef.
3. Cook for 8 hours on low.
4. Shred the beef using 2 forks.

Nutrition facts: 247 Cal, 6 g total fat, 1 g fiber, 40 g protein.

Crush Tomatoes Meaty Bolognese

Ingredients:

Chopped pancetta – 4 ounces

Butter – 1 tablespoon

Minced white onion – 1

Minced celery stalks – 2

Minced carrots – 2

95% lean ground beef – 2 pounds

White wine – ¼ cup

Crushed tomatoes – 2 (28 ounce) cans

Bay leaves – 3

Salt and fresh pepper – To taste

Chopped fresh parsley – ¼ cup

Half & half cream – ½ cup

Directions:

1. Sauté the pancetta in a deep pan for 4-5 minutes on low flame.

2. Add the butter, celery, onions and carrots and cook for around 5 minutes.

3. Increase the flame and add the meat seasoned with salt and pepper, and sauté till browned.

4. Drain the fat and pour in the wine, cooking for 3-4 minutes.

5. Transfer the mixture into the crock pot along with the bay leaves, tomatoes, salt and pepper.

6. Cook covered for 6 hours on low.

7. Mix in the parsley and half & half.

8. Serve over pasta.

Nutrition Information per serving: 143 Cal, 7 g total, 1g fiber, 15 g protein.

Favorite Garlic Bacon & Beef Meatballs

Ingredients:

Ground beef – 2.2 lbs.

Bacon slices (diced) – 2

Onion (quartered) – 1

Garlic cloves – 2

Egg – 1

Salt and pepper – to taste

Favorite herbs – a handful

Canned chopped tomatoes – 14 oz.

Directions:

1. Combine the bacon, onion and garlic in a food processor and process until chopped finely.

2. Mix in the rest of the ingredients except the tomatoes and pulse until you get a smoother paste.

3. Shape the mixture into meatballs and place in a greased slow cooker.

4. Pour over the canned tomatoes.

5. Cook for 4-6 hours on high.

Nutrition facts: 358 Cal, 22 g total fat, 5.2 g carb., 1 g fiber, 33.9 g protein.

Yummy Corned Beef Cabbage Rolls

Ingredients:

Corned beef – 3.5 lbs.

Onion (sliced) – 1

Lemon -1

Coffee – ¼ cup

White wine – ¼ cup

Bacon fat – 1 tablespoon

Brown mustard – 1 tablespoon

Erythritol – 1 tablespoon

Kosher salt – 2 teaspoon

Worcestershire sauce – 2 teaspoon

Peppercorns – 1 teaspoon

Red pepper flakes – ½ teaspoon

Mustard seeds – 1 teaspoon

Cloves – ¼ teaspoon

Allspice – ¼ teaspoon

Bay leaf (crushed) – 1

Savoy cabbage leaves - 15

Directions:

1. Mix together the beef, spices and the liquids to the slow cooker.
2. Cook on low for 6 hours.
3. Bring a pot of water to boil and add the cabbage and onion to it, leaving to boil for 2-3 minutes.
4. Transfer the cabbage leaves into ice cold water for 3-4 minutes. Dry the leaves.
5. Slice the meat and stuff it into the cabbage, rolling it up.
6. Serve with a squeeze of lemon.

Nutrition facts: 478 Cal, 25 g total fat, 3.8 g net. carb., 34.2 g protein.

The One-pot Oriental Lamb

Ingredients:

3 cups lamb, de-boned and diced

2 Tablespoons almond flower

2 cups fresh spinach

4 small red onions, halved

2 garlic cloves, minced

¼ cup yellow turnip, diced

2 Tablespoons dry sherry

2-3 bay leaves

1 teaspoon hot mustard

¼ teaspoon ground nutmeg

1 teaspoon chopped fresh thyme

1 teaspoon chopped fresh rosemary

5-6 whole pimento berries

1⅓ cups broth of your choice – beef, chicken, or lamb

Salt and pepper to taste

8 baby zucchini, halved

2 Tablespoons olive oil

Directions:

1. Preheat the crock-pot on high.

2. Place the lamb in the crock-pot, cover with almond flour. Add the remaining ingredients to crock-pot.

3. Cover, cook on high for 4 hours.

Nutritional facts: net Carb 24g; Protein 50g; Fat 37g, Calories: 510

Serve with green salad and yogurt dressing and fresh chopped dill.

Thyme Beef Pot Roast

Ingredients:

3 pounds beef chuck shoulder roast

2 Tablespoons olive oil

1 red onion, cut into small pieces

1 cup beef broth + 2 cups hot water

4 Tablespoons butter

1 teaspoon dry rosemary

1 teaspoon dry thyme

Salt and pepper to taste

5 medium turnips, peeled, cut into strips

Directions:

1. In a frying pan, heat the olive oil. Brown the meat for 2 minutes on each side.

2. Pour the broth and remaining ingredients, without the turnips, in the crock-pot.

3. Cover, cook on low for 5 hours. Take the lid off and quickly add the turnip strips.

4. Re-cover, cook for an additional 2 hours on low, until the turnips are soft.

Nutritional facts: net Carb 13g; Protein 72g; Fat 26g, Calories: 459

Serve with sour cream and garlic sauce.

CHAPTER 6 DESSERT RECIPES

Cranberry-Apple Dessert

Ingredients:

- 4 apples (medium size; sliced)

- 1 cup cranberries (fresh or frozen)

- 1 tsp vanilla

- 8 tbsp light brown sugar (packed)

- 2 tsp cinnamon (ground)

- 1 x 15 ounces supermoist cake mix (yellow)

- 8 tbsp melted butter

- Whipped cream, as desired

Directions:

1. The slow cooker will be greased.

2. The following ingredients will be added to the slow cooker: cranberries, apples, brown sugar, vanilla, cinnamon (1 tsp). Mix until all the ingredients are well combined.

3. The dry cake mix will be mixed with remaining 1 tsp cinnamon in a different bowl. Spread this mixture over the fruits and drizzle with melted butter.

4. After covering the slow cooker, set the heat on High and cook for about 3 hours. Make sure the fruits are bubbling at edges before ending the cooking process.

5. Serve with whipped cream.

Nutrition facts:

Calories: 230, Fat 12 g, Protein 30g

Pecan Caramel Pudding

Ingredients:

- 1 1/2 cups bisquick mix

- 16 tbsp sugar

- 8 tbsp baking cocoa (make sure it is unsweetened)

- 8 tbsp milk

- 12 tbsp caramel topping

- 1 2/3 cups hot water

- 1/2 cup pecans (chopped; optional ingredient)

Directions:

1. Add the bisquick mix in a large bowl and mix it with 8 tbsp sugar and with cocoa, as well. Add half a cup of the caramel and stir in milk as well. Mix well until all elements are well blended. Transfer the newly obtained mixture into a 3-quart greased slow cooker and pour hot water over it, without any stirring. The remaining sugar will spread over the mixture.

2. After covering the slow cooker, set the heat on Low and cook for 150-180 minutes. Make sure the top center is soft and the top springs back when lightly touched.

3. Let the slow cooker cool uncovered for 15-20 minutes.

4. Spread the remaining caramel (about 4 tbsp) and the chopped pecans on the pudding and serve warm.

Nutrition facts: Calories: 410 ;Total Fat: 6g ;holesterol: 0mg ;Protein: 5g

Chocolate Cake

Ingredients:

1 ½ cups almond flour

¾ cup granulated or powdered sweetener of your choice

⅔ cup cocoa powder

¼ cup whey protein powder

2 teaspoons baking powder

¼ teaspoon salt

½ cup butter, melted (reserve some to brush the crock-pot)

4 large eggs

¾ unsweetened almond milk

1 teaspoon vanilla extract

Directions:

1. In a bowl, mix the dry ingredients.

2. Stir in the wet ingredients one at a time. Combine thoroughly.

3. Butter the crock-pot. Pour in the cake batter.

4. Cover, cook on low for 3 hours. Switch off. Let it set uncovered for 30 minutes.

Nutritional facts: net Carb 4g; Protein 8g; Fat 14g, Calories: 260

Serve with whipped cream and espresso.

Vanilla Peanut Butter Chocolate Cake

Calories:335; Carbs: 11.48g; Fat 27.83g Fiber:5.18g

Ingredients:

- ¾ cup natural peanut butter melted
- 4 eggs
- 2 cups almond flour
- ½ cup water
- ¼ cup unflavored whey protein powder
- ½ cup melted butter
- 2 oz. melted sugar-free dark chocolate
- Sweetener of your choice (use an amount equal to ¾ cup sugar)
- ¼ cup coconut flour
- 1 tsp. vanilla extract
- 1 tbsp. baking powder
- ¼ tsp. salt
- 1 tsp. vanilla extract

Directions:

1. Using butter or cooking spray, grease the inside of your slow cooker.

2. Now, whisk your almond flour, whey protein, coconut flour, salt, and baking powder together. Once well mixed, add in your melted butter, melted peanut butter, vanilla extract, eggs, and water and stir thoroughly.

3. Use a spatula to spoon 2/3 of your batter into the bottom of your slow cooker. Smooth the batter out and then add in half of your melted chocolate. Use the spatula to swirl your chocolate into your batter and then add the rest of your batter to the slow cooker. Put the rest of your chocolate on top and swirl again.

4. Put the lid on your slow cooker and cook on low for 3 ½ to 4 hours until set.

Butter Poppy Seed Cake

Calories: 143; Carbs 9g; Fat 10g; Fiber 1g

Ingredients:

- 4 eggs
- Zest of 4 lemons
- Juice of 4 lemons
- ½ cup melted butter
- 2 cups almond flour
- 3 tbsp. poppy seeds
- 2 tbsp. baking powder
- 1 tbsp. vanilla extract
- 1 tsp. salt
- ¼ cup + 3 tbsp. vanilla protein powder
- ½ cup xylitol

Directions:

1. In a large mixing bowl, combine all of your ingredients except for your eggs together. Once mixed, add your eggs in one at a time and mix thoroughly.

2. Once your ingredients are thoroughly combined, grease your slow cooker with butter or cooking spray.

3. Pour your batter into your slow cooker and smooth over with a spatula.

4. Put the lid on your slow cooker and cook on low for between 2 ½ hours to 3 hours until set.

Almond Raspberry Cake

Calories   362

Carbs 12.76g

Fat   26g

Fiber 6.10g

Ingredients:

- 1 cup fresh raspberries
- 1/3 cup sugar-free dark chocolate chips
- 2 cups almond flour
- 1 tsp. coconut extract
- ¾ cup almond milk
- 4 eggs
- 2 tsp. baking soda
- ¼ tsp. salt
- 1 cup Swerve
- ½ cup melted coconut oil
- 1 cup unsweet shredded coconut
- ¼ cup powdered egg whites

Directions:

1. Begin by greasing your slow cooker with butter or cooking spray.

2. Now, in a large mixing bowl, combine your coconut, almond flour, egg whites, sweetener, salt, and baking soda. Mix well and then stir in your eggs, coconut oil, almond milk, and coconut extract.

3. Once your ingredient mixture is mixed thoroughly, gently fold your chocolate chips and your berries into the ingredients.

4. Spoon your batter into your greased slow cooker and smooth over. Put the lid on your cooker and cook on low for 3 hours until set.

Cocoa Chocolate Cake

Calories   275
Carbs   11.65g
Fat   22.94g
Fiber   5.38g

Ingredients:

- 4 eggs
- 1 ½ cups almond flour
- ½ cup sugar-free chocolate chips
- ¾ cup unsweet almond milk
- 2 tsp. baking powder
- ¼ tsp. salt
- ¼ cup unflavored whey protein powder
- ¾ cup Swerve
- ½ cup melted butter
- 2/3 cup cocoa powder
- 1 tsp. vanilla extract

Directions:

1. Begin by greasing the inside of your slow cooker with butter or cooking spray.

2. Now, in a mixing bowl, combine your cocoa powder, sweetener, almond flour, baking powder, whey protein, salt, and baking powder. Mix well and then add in your eggs, butter, vanilla extract, chocolate chips and almond milk. Stir again to combine.

3. Spoon the batter into your slow cooker and smooth over. Put the lid on your cooker and cook on low for between 2 ½ to 3 hours until set.

4. Let the cake cool completely before cutting and serving.

Best Lemon Cake

Ingredients:

1 ½ cup ground almonds

½ cup coconut flakes

6 Tablespoons sweetener like Swerve (Erythritol, or suitable substitute)

2 teaspoons baking powder

Pinch of salt

½ cup softened coconut oil

½ cup cooking cream

2 Tablespoons lemon juice

Zest from two lemons

2 eggs

Topping:

3 tablespoons Swerve (or suitable substitute)

½ cup boiling water

2 Tablespoons lemon juice

2 Tablespoons softened coconut oil

Directions:

1. In a bowl, combine the almonds, coconut, sweetener, baking powder. Whisk until combined.

2. In a separate bowl, blend coconut oil, cream, juice, and eggs together.

3. Add the egg mixture to the dry ingredients. Mix thoroughly.

4. Line the crock-pot with aluminium foil, pour in the batter.

5. In a bowl, mix the topping. Pour it over the cake batter.

6. Cover the top of the crock-pot with paper towels to absorb the water.

7. Cover, cook on high for 3 hours. Serve warm.

Nutritional values per serving: net Carb 5g; Protein 7g; Fat 24g, Calories: 310

Serve with whipped cream and espresso.

Cream Cheese Pumpkin Cake

Ingredients:

- 1 box yellow cake mix

- 1 cup canned pumpkin

- 8 tbsp water

- 5 tbsp vegetable oil

- 4 eggs

- 1 1/2 tsp pumpkin pie spice

Directions:

1. Using the electric mixer on low speed, beat the eggs, the oil, the water, the pumpkin, the cake mix and the pumpkin pie spice for 1 minute. Make sure you scrape the bowl frequently. Continue to beat for 2 minutes on medium speed.

2. After greasing a slow cooker (5 ½-6 quart), pour the batter inside, set the heat on High and cook for 105-120 minutes. Make sure an inserted toothpick comes out clean before stopping the cooking process. After uncovering the slow cooker, let it cool for 10 minutes. Then, completely remove the cake.

3. In a different bowl, beat the following ingredients with the electric mixer on low speed: butter, cream cheese and vanilla. Stop the beating process when the mixture is smooth. Add powdered sugar, as well (only 1 cup at a time) and continue to beat, using the electric mixer on low speed. Stop the beating process when the mixture is smooth. Spread over the cake. You can sprinkle some walnuts or pecans, too.

Nutrition Information:

Calories: 290 ;Total Fat: 13g ;Protein: 3g

Dark Chocolate Raspberry Cake

Ingredients:

2 cups ground almonds

1 cup shredded coconut

¾ cup sweetener, Swerve (or suitable substitute)

2 teaspoon baking soda

¼ teaspoon salt

4 large eggs

½ cup melted coconut oil

¾ cup coconut milk

1 cup raspberries, fresh or frozen

½ cup sugarless dark chocolate chips

Directions:

1. Butter the crock-pot. In a bowl, mix the dry ingredients.

3. Beat in the eggs, melted coconut oil, and coconut milk. Gently fold in the raspberries and chocolate chips.

4. Combine the cocoa, almonds, and salt in a bowl.

5. Pour the batter into the buttered crock-pot.

6. Cover the crock-pot with a paper towel to absorb the water.

7. Cover, cook on low for 3 hours. Let the cake cool in the pot.

Nutritional facts: net Carb 8g; Protein 7g; Fat 23g , Cal:310

Serve with whipped coconut cream and espresso.

Cheesy Red Velvet Cake

Ingredients:

- 1 box devil's food cake mix

- water (check the above mentioned box instructions)

- oil (check the above mentioned box instructions)

- eggs (check the above mentioned box instructions)

- 1 ounce red food color

- 1 container creamy cream cheese frosting

Directions:

1. A 5-quart slow cooker will be used here. The sides and the bottom of the slow cooker will be lined with cooking parchment paper and greased, too (use cooking spray for this purpose).

2. Follow the instructions on the box in order to make the cake batter. Make sure you add food color with water, too.

3. The batter will be transferred and folded in the slow cooker. A clean dish towel will be placed under the cover of the slow cooker. This is needed in order to stop the condensation from dripping over the batter.

4. Set the heat on High and cook for 3 quarters of an hour. Remove the ceramic insert of your slow cooker and rotate insert 180 degrees. Make sure you leave the cover on. Cook for another 45-60 minutes. Stop the cooking process when an inserted toothpick comes out clean.

5. Remove the ceramic insert and place it on a cooling rack. Let it cool for about 10 minutes.

6. Remove the cake from the ceramic insert (use parchment paper). Place it on the cooling rack and let it cool for about 60 minutes.

7. The frosting will be spread over the cake.

Nutrition Information:

Calories: 380

Total Fat: 17g

Protein: 1g

Coconut Carrot Cake

Calories : 348

Carbs: 9.5g

Fat: 20g

Fiber: 4.14g

Ingredients:

- 4 eggs at room temperature
- 2 cups grated carrots
- 1 ½ cups almond flour
- 3 tbsp. almond milk
- ¼ tsp. salt
- 2 tsp. baking powder
- ¼ cup melted coconut oil
- ¼ cup unflavored whey protein powder
- ½ cup shredded coconut
- ½ cup chopped walnuts
- ¾ cup Swerve sweetener
- 1 tsp. ground cinnamon
- ¼ tsp. ground cloves
- ½ tsp. vanilla extract

Cream Cheese Frosting

- 6 oz. softened cream cheese

- ¾ tsp. vanilla extract

- ½ cup room temperature heavy cream

- ½ cup powdered sweetener

Directions:

1. Grease the inside of your slow cooker using butter or cooking spray. Once greased, line the sides of the cooker with parchment paper and grease that too.

2. Now, in a large mixing bowl, combine your almond flour, coconut, sweetener, nuts, baking powder, protein powder, cloves, cinnamon, and salt. Mix together these ingredients thoroughly and then stir in your eggs, carrots, almond milk, coconut oil, and vanilla extract. Mix again to combine again and then spread in the bottom of your slow cooker.

3. Put the lid on your slow cooker and cook for 3 hours to 3 ½ hours on low until your cake is set through.

4. Turn your cake out onto a cooling rack to cool completely. While your cake cools, combine your powdered sweetener and cream cheese in a small mixing bowl. Mix together well and then mix in your cream and vanilla extract.

5. When your ingredients are well mixed, and your cake has cooled thoroughly, spread the icing on top of your cake and serve!

Butter Almond Cocoa Cake

Ingredients:

¾ cup butter, melted

1 ½ cups powdered sweetener

⅔ cup Dutch cocoa powder

⅓ cup ground almonds

Pinch of salt

3 large eggs

1 teaspoon vanilla

½ cup dark chocolate chips

Directions:

1. Line the crock-pot with aluminium foil and butter it.
2. In a bowl, mix all the ingredients.
3. Pour the batter into the buttered crock-pot.
4. Cover the pot with a paper towel to absorb the water.
5. Cover, cook on low for 3 hours.

Nutritional values per serving: net Carb 3g; Protein 6g; Fat 21g, Calories: 245

Serve with whipped cream and espresso.

Coconut Blueberry Crisp

Calories 352

Carbs 29.4g

Fat 25.1g

Fiber 5.1g

Ingredients:

- 24 oz. frozen blueberries
- ¾ cup almond flour
- ¼ cup melted coconut oil
- ¼ cup melted butter
- 1 ½ cups rolled oats
- ¼ cup granulated sugar substitute
- 2 tbsp. brown sugar
- 1 cup chopped pecans
- ¾ tsp. salt

Directions:

1. Begin by greasing your slow cooker with butter or cooking spray.
2. Add your blueberries to the bottom of your slow cooker.

3. Now, add your rolled oats to your food processor and chop them until you get a small grind but not too small. Empty this grind out into a small bowl and add your butter, coconut oil, and nuts.

4. Next, add in your flour, sweetener, salt, and brown sugar. Stir to mix everything together thoroughly. Spread this topping mixture on top of your blueberries in your slow cooker.

5. Place a clean kitchen towel or paper towels on top of your cooker to catch condensation.

6. Cover your slow cooker and cook on high heat for between 3 and 4 hours or until your berries are tender, and the mixture is boiling. Serve hot!

Vanilla Chocolate Cheesecake

Ingredients:

3 cups cream cheese

Pinch of salt

3 eggs

1 cup powder sweetener of your choice, Swerve (or suitable substitute)

1 teaspoon vanilla extract

½ cup sugarless dark chocolate chips

Directions:

1. In a bowl, beat together the cream cheese, sweetener, and salt.

2. Add the eggs one at a time. Combine thoroughly.

3. Spread the cheesecake in a cake pan, which fits in the crock-pot you are using.

4. Melt the chocolate chips in a small pot and pour over the batter. Using a knife, swirl the chocolate through the batter.

5. Pour 2 cups of water in the crock-pot and set the cake pan inside. Attention: Careful the water does not exceed the level of the cake pan.

6. Cover the pot with a paper towel to absorb the water.

7. Cover, cook on high for 2.5 hours. Remove from the crock-pot and let it cool in the pan for 1 hour. Refrigerate.

Nutritional facts: net Carb 3g; Protein 8g; Fat 26g , Cal: 365

Double Crème Brûlée

Ingredients:

5 large egg yolks

6 Tablespoons sweetener, Erythritol

2 cups double cream

1 Bourbon vanilla pod, scraped

Pinch of salt

Directions:

1. In a bowl, beat the eggs and sweetener together.

2. Add the cream and vanilla. Whisk together.

3. Divide the mixture between 6 small ramekin dishes or one big dish.

4. Set them in the crock-pot and pour hot water around them - so the water reaches half way up the ramekins.

5. Cover, cook on high for 2 hours.

6. Take the dishes out, let them cool. Refrigerate for 6-8 hours.

Nutritional facts: net Carb 2g; Protein 2g; Fat 24g , Calories: 372

Serve with whipped cream and espresso.

Nutmeg Coconut-Peach Cobbler

Calories   192

Carbs   13.5g

Fat   10.3g

Fiber   2.5g

Ingredients:

- 6 cups fresh sliced peaches
- 1 tbsp. honey
- 1/8 tbsp. nutmeg
- ½ tbsp. cinnamon
- 1/8 tsp. salt

Topping:

- 4 eggs
- 2 tbsp. almond milk
- ¼ cup coconut oil
- 2 ½ tbsp. honey
- 1 cup almond flour
- 1/3 cup coconut flour
- 1/8 tsp. salt

- 1 tsp. baking powder
- ¼ tsp. almond extract

Directions:

1. Begin by greasing your slow cooker using butter or cooking spray.

2. Next, add your non-topping ingredients to a bowl and mix together thoroughly. Spread this mixture in the bottom of your slow cooker.

3. Now start your topping. In a large mixing bowl, mix together your flours, salt, and baking powder.

4. In another bowl, combine your coconut oil, eggs, almond extract, almond milk, and honey. Stir to combine them and then slowly mix this mixture into your flour mixture. Once thoroughly combined, spoon this mix on top of your peaches.

5. Put the lid on your slow cooker and cook for between 4 and 6 hours on low heat until bubbling and the topping is set. Serve hot!

Almond Berry & Coconut Cake

Ingredients:

1 Tablespoon butter for greasing the crock

1 cup almond flour

¾ cup sweetener of your choice

1 teaspoon baking soda

¼ teaspoon salt

1 large egg, beaten with a fork

¼ cup coconut flour

¼ cup coconut milk

2 Tablespoons coconut oil

4 cups fresh or frozen blueberries and raspberries

Directions:

1. Butter the crock-pot well.

2. In a bowl, whisk the egg, coconut milk, and oil together.

3. Mix the dry ingredients. Slowly stir in the wet ingredients. Do not over mix.

4. Pour the batter in the crock-pot, spread evenly.

5. Spread the berries on top.

6. Cover, cook on high for 2 hours. Cool in the crock for 1-2 hours.

Nutritional facts: net Carb 7g; Protein 7g; Fat 17g ; Calories: 268

Whey Vanilla Pudding Cake

Ingredients:

1 Tablespoon butter for greasing the crock-pot

1 ½ cups ground almonds

¾ cup sweetener, Swerve (or a suitable substitute)

¾ cup cocoa powder

¼ cup whey protein

2 teaspoons baking powder

¼ teaspoon salt

4 large eggs

½ cup butter, melted

¾ cup full-fat cream

1 teaspoon vanilla extract

Directions:

1. Butter the crock-pot thoroughly.
2. In a bowl, whisk the dry ingredients together.
3. Stir in the melted butter, eggs, cream, and vanilla. Mix well.
4. Pour the batter into the crock-pot and spread evenly.
5. Cover, cook on low for 2½ to 3 hours. If preferred – more like pudding, cook cake shorter; more dry cake, cook longer.
6. Cool in the crock-pot for 30 minutes. Cut and serve.

Nutritional facts: net Carb 4.5g; Protein 10g; Fat 12g , Calories : 210

Conclusion

Thank you so much again for downloading this book!

I hope the recipes in this book will amaze you and will help you lose weight fast

Finally, if you enjoyed this book would you be kind enough to leave a review for this book on Amazon? It'd be greatly appreciated!

Thank you and good luck!

Made in the USA
Lexington, KY
18 August 2017